SHOOTING AND CUTTING

SHOOTING
AND
CUTTING

A SURVIVOR'S GUIDE TO
FILM-MAKING AND OTHER DISEASES

STEPHEN BRADLEY

MERCIER PRESS

MERCIER PRESS

Cork

www.mercierpress.ie

© Stephen Bradley, 2019

Back cover photograph © Destiny Films

ISBN: 978 1 78117 676 4

A CIP record for this title is available from the British Library.

Printed and bound in the EU.

In memory of Dr Fiona Bradley
1961–2002

Much of this book was written under the influence of opiates, steroids, antibiotics, benzodiazepines, antiemetics, chemotherapy, immunotherapy, with bouts of cold turkey, and sharp injections of love and good luck.

'The day is now well advanced. And yet it is perhaps a little soon for my song. To sing too soon is fatal, I always find. On the other hand, it is possible to leave it too late. The bell goes for sleep and one has not sung.'

– Winnie in *Happy Days* by Samuel Beckett

CONTENTS

MONDAY, 18 APRIL 2016

I am anxious.

I leave a large Victorian house in Dublin and cross the road. It is freezing cold. More than it should be for this time of year. I walk parallel to a line of black iron railings and focus my eyes beyond them into a wintry park. It's an unexceptional tracking shot.

I took up residence here three weeks ago, departing London after ten years to begin the next part of my family's journey, back in our native Ireland. We can't afford the crazy rent for the house, but we've been offered places at an excellent local school and have thrown caution to the wind. The days since we arrived have been chock-a-block. Our children, Holly and Daniel, aged eleven and seven respectively, have needed to be settled in and convinced of the wisdom of a sudden move across the Irish Sea. My wife has been busy preparing for, then subsequently hosting, a live broadcast of the Irish Film and Television Awards. Deirdre O'Kane, actress, stand-up comic and television presenter, has a gratifying level of notoriety throughout the country. She is much in demand, and has gone away for a couple of days to record a radio play in Belfast.

I am still walking beside the railings.

Still anxious.

Since my return, several people have told me that I don't look my usual self. How could I look my usual self, I reason, when I've just packed up a London family and speedily converted it into a Dublin one, all in a matter of weeks? That's a lot of boxes and furniture heaved into a removal lorry. Plus a long drive with a terrified English cat, who then proved determined to escape across the deck of an Irish ferry in the middle of the night.

Upheavals aside, apparently I just don't look healthy. So I am on my way to a doctor's surgery. I leave behind the frosty park and head downhill towards the sea, where a stone pier stretches out into the bay.

Naturally, I tell Dr McSwiney a few select but enthralling details about my family's international transfer. His youthful face is open and kind but discourages further small talk. I reluctantly admit to feeling exhausted and I report some unusual digestive issues that have emerged during the past couple of weeks. I helpfully suggest stress as a possible cause.

The doctor starts prodding and poking. He sticks a digital thermometer into my ear. 'You've got a temperature of 102. That's high.' He places a hand beneath my ribs. 'And I can feel that your liver is swollen. I could prescribe you some antibiotics for a week, but I don't think they would make any difference. I want you to go to the Accident and Emergency

Department at The Hospital, without delay, and I'll give you a letter of introduction to hand in at reception.'

I immediately feel faint, requiring a glass of water and a lie-down in my new doctor's office. It's nice to meet you; please accept my apologies for the fact that I'm already threatening to collapse onto your faded Persian rug.

Something is wrong with the body that I have taken for granted for too long. I breathe deeply, reminding myself that I am a catastrophic thinker, and so try to stop my thoughts in mid-gloom.

Everything will be fine.

BEGINNING

It was two birthdays later, at the end of August 2017, that I took possession of myself again. I had spent too many long days in our vast but comforting old bedroom, with a high ceiling that made it impossible to heat during the five darkest months. The same space where the sun's embers had often electrified my doubting soul at magic hour, as a couple of tough summers passed me by. I was remade into a child in that room. Now, entering adulthood once more, I knew that I had to take my leave of this sanctuary.

So I did.

According to the ancient traditions of storytelling, I should have returned from my ordeal with a hero's boon: the wisdom gained from a long journey across uncharted, obstacle-strewn lands; or, better still, by the rules of lore, I should have carried a tangible pot of gold in my newly restored and muscular arms. Neither of those rewards had been bestowed upon me. Because, as poor old Michael Finnegan will tell you in that famous children's song, if there's one thing more difficult than to begin, it's to begin again.

A screenplay arrived unannounced out of the great wide blue. It was written by a man I didn't know particularly well. Nor did I know why he had sent it to me, of all people. I read it straight away, which I never do. It was called *The Safe*.

I loved the first third of the story and my heartbeat quickened as I turned the pages. Then it lost its way and lost me too. But I didn't write it off completely. Because I was, latish on in life, finally coming to terms with the demands of traversing creative minefields. I now understood some of the complex calculations involved: adding talent to blood, sweat and tears, multiplying by serendipity and subtracting expectation to equal a total of uncertainty.

'Please give me a very honest reaction,' the screenwriter said.

So I did.

Wrote him some notes. Critical, constructive and to the point.

He called me a bastard.

It was a joke.

This screenwriter, this man I didn't know particularly well, was also a stand-up comic. One of the most respected on a comedy circuit that I had haunted for twenty years or more as a consequence of my marriage. In addition, this performer, who once possessed a natural shock of the reddest hair imaginable, was the author of fine poetry, numerous plays, a television series or three, and a film directed by a name you would definitely know.

His hair was greyer now because he was older and wiser.

Secretly, he liked my bastard notes.

He asked if I would read another draft of the script in a few months' time.

I said yes. I would.

With good reason.

Because one of the main twists in the story was an uncanny reflection of something that had happened in my own life. Clearly, I can't reveal what the dramatic moment was, for I would be guilty of that most modern of mortal sins – the spoiler. But the extraordinary coincidence struck me as a good reason to engage. Sometimes the decision to proceed with the long and arduous task of developing a screenplay turns on such a personal connection. And obviously, I knew a lot about that strand of the story, from first-hand experience, so I thought that I could bring a new energy to help the writer with his endeavours.

I sent him an email, revealing those dark secrets of mine that chimed with his script.

'Fucking hell!' he wrote poetically in reply. 'If that isn't a good omen, I don't know what is.'

The writer had a name. Owen O'Neill.

His screenplay had already moved me to tears.

STILL MONDAY, 18 APRIL 2016

I am in an old taxi as it rattles along the bus lanes towards The Hospital. Deirdre won't be back from her radio job until tomorrow, so I activate the contingency grandparents option. Pamela and Brendan agree to pick our children up from their new school and await further instructions.

In the first of many coincidences that are about to grace my life over the coming months, my sister Suzie's office is a five-minute walk from the main entrance to The Hospital. I ring her to explain the situation and she promises that she will visit me as soon as I have signed in and presented my swollen liver. I feel a little better already, if only because wheels are in motion. Hopefully I'll be in and out pronto, maybe even cooking fish fingers by teatime. The taxi driver, clearly knowing more than I do, issues a very serious 'Good luck, pal' message as he swings to a stop outside the A&E.

I take another deep breath as I breach the double doors. There is only one family waiting ahead of me, an unusual occurrence in such a busy wing of The Hospital. Half of that family's members are pacing up and down, still in their dressing gowns. The other half are trying to find out who left the tablets lying around at home, thereby facilitating the attempted suicide of a loved one. Tears and recriminations suddenly surround and unsettle me.

I am soon called into the triage unit, where a Malaysian doctor confirms my high temperature and predicts that I will need treatment for a liver infection. I won't be going home today either, I am informed, as there are tests and examinations to undergo. I am nevertheless satisfied and relieved that the ailment sounds easily treatable, and so I settle into prime position on trolley number one. By the time Suzie arrives with an *Irish Times* newspaper and sandwiches for lunch, I am being hooked up to my second bag of intravenous saline fluid to combat dehydration. I have also been scheduled for an afternoon appointment with the computed tomography (CT) scanning machine.

The A&E is now busy, noisy and uncomfortably airless. The triage team has filled trolley number thirty-five. There is a member of An Garda Síochána in attendance to enforce a barring order against the father of a patient. The errant dad is roaming the department, looking for a chance to cross the barricades.

When the nurses' shift change happens at 8 p.m., I am relieved to have my own trolley wheeled into a windowless grey cell that seems to me to have all the privacy of a plush hotel. My sister stays with me as late as is humanly permitted. There's a reason why her childhood nickname was 'Suzie Angel'.

Then I'm on my own.

In the middle of the night, rupturing my already uncertain and trolley-bound sleep, a ghostly figure arrives to cart me off for a chest X-ray. I make no protest, not knowing whether this is real or a dream.

In the early morning, everything comes into sharp focus as the doors of my cell are suddenly blasted wide open. The gastroenterologist enters like the wind, energetic and forceful, with three junior doctors in desperate pursuit. I sit up, startled and bleary-eyed. There follows an interrogation. An inquisition. From the gastroenterologist's point of view, there is an urgent necessity for information.

'Do you drink a lot? Who do you drink with? When? Do you drink spirits? How much does your wife drink? How often would you drink a bottle of wine? How many nights a week do you drink? Are you a secret drinker? Is this your first time in hospital recently?'

She immediately has me on the ropes and I mumble my answers with embarrassment in front of the all-female posse. When they leave (after listing all the future tests that are going to conclusively and unavoidably expose me as a substance abuser) I have already convinced myself that I must indeed drink to excess. Up to this point I hadn't believed that I ever consistently consumed too much in the way of alcoholic beverages, but it is possible that I have been deluding myself. Perhaps I have, in part, even returned back to Ireland to escape what everyone in London has been saying about me behind my back for years: that I am a chronic secret drinker?

It hasn't taken long to make me doubt myself and become paranoid. That's the level of vulnerability I am feeling inside the cell's grey walls, now closing inexorably in on me.

By the time Deirdre returns from Belfast, I am full of apologies for having apparently thrown my life away on the booze. If there is something seriously wrong with me I will only have myself to blame and I will have wasted my opportunity to fulfil the role of husband and father, let alone son or brother. I am a pathetic wreck.

Deirdre almost slaps me back to my senses. You do not drink to excess by any normal standard, she berates me. And, as the blood tests and scan results start to roll in, the gastroenterologist, whose name is Juliette Sheridan, also realises that I am not a practising alcoholic, but more like a scared mid-lifer who is prepared to consider a false confession under duress. She gives me strong intravenous antibiotics to battle various digestive infections, and pinky blood products to lift my iron levels.

Over a period of forty-eight hours I begin to feel human again. Dr Sheridan is immediately caring, charming, expert and attentive. There is some undefined quality about her that is reassuring to behold. For the next week, I am going to be under her care while the gastroenterology team resurrects my system.

But, for now, we make two clear discoveries together: firstly that, in a strange coincidence, she and her family live four doors along from our newly rented house; and secondly that, while it is true that I have plenty of the predicted infection throughout my digestive tract, there is also something more alarming in play.

The CT scan shows a shadow covering half of my liver.

It indicates an abnormal growth of large and worrying proportions.

REAPPEARING

After my long stretch of treatment, it was vital for me to rebuild a head of steam with my work during the winter months of 2017. In this business, that rarely happened either quickly or smoothly. Development was often referred to as hell. Productions could falter or collapse. Distribution, if you were fortunate enough to get that far, was often a disappointment.

Like many film-makers, I had enjoyed some minor victories and successes in the past. But on other occasions I had also lost my confidence, or pursued ideas that weren't strong enough to survive such a competitive arena. Even though I was not a prolific writer-director, I had been involved in enough projects to experience that dark triumvirate of hell, collapse and disappointment. In spite of all this, and following in the path of every dewy-eyed gambler before me, I was keen to roll the dice again.

I had made my last film, *Noble*, four years previously, in 2013. It was based on the true story of the eponymous Christina Noble, an Irishwoman of exceptional abilities and colourful characteristics. It followed her dramatic journey from tough beginnings in Ireland and Britain to selfless achievements in the protection and nurture of thousands upon thousands of street-children in Vietnam and Mongolia. When the film was finished, I travelled with it extensively, screened it incessantly, and question-and-answered for audiences until my saliva and energy ran dry. Then, as far as most of the world was concerned, I had simply disappeared.

I needed to stage a re-emergence. I also wanted to see if I could get my creative juices flowing again. For the previous two years, my other bodily fluids had been the only talking point.

As I went out in public once more, people were either shocked to see me, or hadn't noticed my absence because time passes so swiftly and I was distant on their social radar in any case as a result of our lengthy escape to England and my subsequent illness. I found crowds difficult at the beginning. I felt like my explanations as to what had happened were in danger of being considered unnecessary, repetitive or simply unwelcome to my listeners.

During my malaise, there had been a cohort of the close and the loyal who had walked with me along the stone pier out into Dublin Bay as my levels of strength waxed and waned. Among those friends were some of my favourite directors, composers, actors, production designers and writers. I had tested ideas out on them; images, pitches, soundscapes and themes had been discussed. My companions rolled with my meanderings and encouraged all manner of fantasies. But real, feasible, practical plans for film or television productions were still a way out to sea, some distance beyond the curvature.

Ordinariness also made an extraordinarily welcome return during this period. I enjoyed my children, laughed with my wife, prepared to renovate a house that we had recently bought. I wrote satisfying notes and scenes, obsessively organising files into flocks and formations on my treasured laptop. I made phone calls, wrote emails and tweeted. For pleasure. I engaged in such complicated tasks as school runs, supermarket shops, swims, ambitious culinary exercises, holiday plans and homework. All were exotic activities to the new me.

The weather was the only thing that was sub-par. In fact, it was abysmal. The quantity of rain and snow that fell caused a nationwide fodder crisis and necessitated the importation of supplies to save Ireland's livestock. Freezing storms brought wind and whiteness, and shut the country down. Ice cracked the porcelain of our attic toilet. I survived all of that. I must have been ready for action.

The new draft screenplay of *The Safe* arrived. It was full of fresh storylines, intriguing characters, seams of comedy, visual flourishes and, most importantly, an emotional and cathartic punch in the gut at the finish. Of course, it wasn't perfect. No director or producer has ever said that a script didn't constantly need more work. But I thought it was perfect enough for me to tell Owen O'Neill that I liked it. Expressed in carefully measured terms, you understand, so that I wouldn't swell his head and make him a pain in the arse to work with.

Agents were called and deal memos signed.

Development funding was sought and decisions were awaited.

I was back in the game.

WEDNESDAY, 20 APRIL 2016

The shadow on my liver comes under severe scrutiny.

This culminates in a biopsy guided by ultrasound. I have been warned that this can be a very painful procedure, so I encourage the use of as much local anaesthetic as possible, and the ultrasound man obliges. I have my stomach smeared with gel as if I'm pregnant, which in an *Alien* (dir. Ridley Scott, 1979) sort of way I am. Surprisingly, there's no pain at all during the biopsy. Instead, just the very weird sensation of cores of tissue being pulled out of my liver, like little corks.

My diagnosis is left unsaid for now. But there is a tacit understanding. After all, I have met the liver surgeon, Dr Justin Geoghegan (another patient later refers to him admiringly as 'Gold Fingers') and we have discussed vague possibilities. He is a wonderfully lithe, considered and gentle man. Bizarrely, I am told that he lives three doors down from our newly rented house, right next to Juliette Sheridan. Justin confirms this to be true.

'No pressure then,' I jest feebly.

He smiles a wry one, undoubtedly wishing that I would shut up. But what does a nervously uttered *faux pas* matter under these circumstances? All that I care about is that he has the reputation for being a fantastically skilful practitioner, one of the very best. Which is just as well, because I am a public patient and not a private one. Where most people in Britain rely solely on the National Health Service (NHS), there is a different culture in Ireland, where private health insurance is largely seen as essential if a family can manage to afford it. As we have made the move home from London so quickly, our uncompleted insurance forms still sit accusingly on top of the to-do pile of papers in the kitchen. There's no hope of insuring me now.

Juliette Sheridan is the first to address this state of affairs, and what she says is surprising. She tells me that she knows I will have heard, particularly coming from NHS-land, that the public system here is weak, straining at the seams and anxiety-inducing for patients. However, she says frankly, as a generalisation that is simply not true. Juliette assures me that I am going to get the very best care here in the Irish public health system. Her words could not have been more reassuring or, as it turns out, prescient. I will ever be thankful for that and I am also painfully aware that there are many places in the world where, uninsured, I wouldn't have stood a chance.

My medical team informs me that I am to be allowed home for some hours during the weekend, even though I will have to spend my nights on the ward. We can discuss tactics on Monday, they say, once the liver biopsy results are in.

Meanwhile, I am lucky to have been moved from my grey cell in A&E to a spacious, well-equipped single room, with a window overlooking the adjacent golf course. In truth, the doctors are carefully weaving some space and time for Deirdre and myself to be together at home with our children, Holly and Daniel. Because they know what is likely to be ahead.

***

On the other hand, there is no way that my good friend Stephen Rennicks can suspect what is likely to be ahead of me. Stephen has just returned from Los Angeles, where he attended the Oscars to celebrate the success of *Room* (dir. Lenny Abrahamson, 2014), for which he composed the musical score. He and I have been pals for many years, but haven't seen much of each other while I was based in London. Our life partners have remained very close since their teenage years (and are confusingly both called Deirdre), but distance is distance and it has been difficult for us all to get together in person. Still, on hearing of my hospitalisation, Stephen gets in touch by text:

> *Steve, sorry to hear you're in hospital. Let me know if there's anything you need … really. X Steve*

My response:

> *Thanks Stevo, not really sure how this is going to pan out, will stick with all the tests for the next few days. I'll def call on you if I need company. Are you working on a big film at the moment? Xx*

His reply:

> *No big film, managed to dodge one recently. Lots of lovely smaller projects going. Hospital is a lonely place so I may not wait for your call but I'll leave it a couple of days anyway.*

That final phrase strikes me as being strangely presumptuous. How can Stephen Rennicks know that I'll be lonely, or what my visiting needs will be beyond the support of my immediate family? Well, if he ever wants to be presumptuous again in the future, he can presume away, any time he likes. Because, as it turns out, he is about to be there for me during every late and lonely hospital evening of what are possibly the hardest twelve days of my life. Just as Deirdre and I are about to experience one of the worst weekends that we will ever be forced to endure.

***

Late on Friday, I have a colonoscopy to investigate the state of my large colon and to check for signs of diverticulitis, an inflammation of the lining. While this is not performed under a general anaesthetic, there is an appreciable and appreciated quantity of drug relief administered, to disguise what can be a painful and intrusive procedure.

Beforehand, I can sense high spirits among the various medical staff in the small operating theatre. The Hospital, even more than most work places, undergoes a definite change on a Friday afternoon. Doctors and nurses are coming to the end of another tough week dealing with life and, occasionally, death. There's an understandable lift of mood. Perhaps even giddiness. In spite of this I become aware, through the anaesthetic haze, that extra attention is being paid to me during the procedure by a growing number of attending medics. I decide that it is part of the sociable Friday atmosphere and I don't enquire further once the wooziness wears off. Denial is a powerful force.

The Hospital continues to shed staff. A skeleton crew of nurses and a reduced dose of doctors take charge for the weekend hours. From a patient's point of view it's a noticeable and not altogether welcome change for the simple reason that treatment and attention, the dual currencies of your existence, are harder to come by.

Deirdre and I hold hands like teenagers as we lie side by side on the bed in my single room overlooking the eighth green of the golf course adjacent to The Hospital. The last golfers pass by outside in late-afternoon April showers. We complete the newspaper crossword puzzle together, one of several distractions we have already made into a habit. Dee (as she came to call herself in England when people couldn't pronounce the longer version of her Irish name) will soon leave to look after our children for the evening. So these are valuable moments to us.

Suddenly the door flies open and a doctor strides into the room. We have never met him before, although he was apparently one of the team in the colonoscopy department, so I may have glimpsed him earlier through the haze. He asks us if we would like to know what he has discovered, telling us that if he were in our situation he would want to know. He also enquires whether or not we would like to see the photographs that were taken during the procedure. Before we have time to respond, he lays the graphic images out on the bed. I look down to see ugly, black, shiny tissue dominating the frame. The doctor explains that they are pictures of my bowel cancer.

I know at this moment, with a final admission to myself, that the shadow on my liver is also definitely a large cancer.

All the blood drains from my head.

I realise there and then that I am probably going to die. And soon.

I know that, logically speaking, my whole body must be

wracked by this disease. Whatever bravery my wife and I can muster will now be in the context of a final reckoning. Like me, Deirdre is extraordinarily distressed, but she is also angry with the blunt, matter-of-fact way the news has been delivered.

She faces the doctor down:

'I want you to say something positive before you leave. You have come into the room on a Friday evening and taken it upon yourself to tell us all this. We don't know who you are. Now you're just going to walk out and leave us to try to process this news. Because obviously we now know that the growth on Stephen's liver will not be benign. I want you to say something positive to us. So that you are not just deserting us here in the darkness.'

The doctor is undoubtedly taken aback by Deirdre's show of strength, and also by her ability to insist that a negative conclusion will not be countenanced. He stutters a little and tells us the details of a case that he remembers, involving a combination of these two cancers and a patient who is still healthy, a decade after treatment. Then he beats a rapid retreat.

***

On Sunday morning, the weather is dry and not excessively cold. I take a taxi home from The Hospital for the first time. It is the strangest of feelings as the car turns towards our rented house, which stands in the middle of an impressive period terrace. The walls of these buildings are old and they have tales to tell of the generations that have come and gone. The majestic chestnut trees in front of them have their own stories, locked into each annual growth ring. I try to grasp at these thoughts of time passing, as if I have some forlorn hope that I might change time's course and rewind it. Since I was last here, all of five days ago, my perception of this beautiful little domestic world has altered completely.

We walk our children to a popular local park, where artisan food stalls and coffee tents are set out in rows. Our little family huddles together at the base of a tree with our takeaway meals. Deirdre and I try to disguise our thoughts by chatting with Holly and Daniel, answering their myriad questions about school, friends, life and the universe as best we can.

We even manage some forced smiles.

But mostly we just clutch at each other, attempting to deal with our joint and separate despair.

We are more lost than we have ever been.

Periodically, one of us finds some pale words of comfort.

And says them.

DRIVING

2018 arrived. I was on parole in the real world, under the supervision of my oncologist, and was still uncomfortably disorientated by the normal challenges of life and living. I had cooked Christmas dinner for eight family members, and struggled with my supervisory duties on the renovation of the quirky house we had purchased. These tasks, and the early morning school run with Holly and Daniel, seemed to be the height of my capabilities. I certainly wasn't earning any money, so Deirdre continued to shoulder that responsibility. She took a job as a contestant on a television show, *Dancing with the Stars*, and excelled all the way to the final of the competition over twelve gruelling weeks of live performances. It provided us with a mid-winter focus, although Deirdre's constant absence from home also, selfishly, gave me something to complain about. Occasionally, I surprised myself with my own churning annoyance and negativity, like a counterbalance to all the positive energy we had summoned as an extended family to lift me out of the mental and physical doldrums during my long illness.

When I was on my own, I sometimes drove too fast.

As a state of being. As a pathetic protest.

Fortunately I wasn't driving fast, or at all, when I received a phone call from Sir George Martin's manager, Adam Sharp. I hadn't been in touch with Adam for exactly two years. Not since Deirdre and I had been forced to turn down his invitation to attend George's memorial service at the aptly named St Martin-in-the-Fields, in London. I was newly ensconced in The Hospital at the time, in the first days after my diagnosis, so there was no chance of us being there.

Deirdre and I had become close to the Martin family during our decade living in England. One of the many happy results of the friendship was that George's son, Giles, composed the music for our film *Noble*. His wife, Melanie Gore-Grimes, had previously been a locations scout on my first attempt as writer-director, *Sweety Barrett* (1998). Much more recently, she had undertaken the mammoth task of producing *Noble*, as we filmed on opposite sides of the world in Liverpool and Saigon. After that shoot, we were all working together at Abbey Road Studios on the day that the orchestra recorded the score. George Martin stopped by his old haunt to see us, on a rare and unannounced visit. I remember looking down from the mixing room onto Studio One, as the accomplished musicians, notoriously hard to impress, broke into spontaneous applause when they saw The Beatles' producer.

The Martins generously lent us their remote stone cottage, an hour's drive from London, for much-needed weekend breaks. It had originally been acquired as George and Judy's escape from the Beatlemania that enveloped their lives during the Swinging Sixties. Our young children enjoyed going there so they could roam free. To me, it was blissful. On warm summer evenings, we used to wander along a dusty track, through fields of cows, then on up the hill to a much larger rectory house that the Martins had purchased in the 1970s, where we would join them for drinks and dinner.

In 2011, I had cast George in his film-acting debut, playing the older version of Cillian Murphy's character in my French wartime thriller, *Wayfaring Strangers.* George had trained as a flyer with the Fleet Air Arm in 1945, so he had a more direct connection to my story than anyone else involved. I was excited and gratified when he agreed to play the part.

As for Cillian, his involvement had provided the final momentum that any production needs, in the push towards what is known as First Day of Principal Photography. It was the year after *Inception* (dir. Christopher Nolan) was released, and Cillian's prominent role in that blockbuster didn't do our cause any harm.

His very first film part had been in my own debut, the aforementioned *Sweety Barrett*, produced by Ed Guiney, my partner in Temple Films. (Ironically, it was also a co-production with Handmade Films, the company founded by the Beatle George Harrison.) Ed had gone on to make the screen adaptation of Enda Walsh's play *Disco Pigs* (dir. Kirsten Sheridan, 1999), which was Cillian's first leading role on screen. So his enthusiastic support for *Wayfaring Strangers* had been sort of a payback, with a load of compound interest piled on top.

George Martin's short section of the film was set during the present day. It saw him travelling by Eurostar to Gare du Nord in Paris, and continuing south to Burgundy by car. In the screenplay, George's voice-over accompanied flashbacks to the main story. Cillian Murphy was then called on for the heavy lifting, depicting his character's younger self during dramatic and dangerous wartime events in 1942.

Cillian recently told me that, when he arrived in the Burgundy town of Montbard to prepare for the start of filming, he had a feeling that it was going to be one of the best films he ever made. That compliment meant a huge amount to me, particularly in the context of what happened next.

The production financing for *Wayfaring Strangers* collapsed at the final hour, of the final day, of the final week of preparations. We were poised and ready to shoot. Cillian had even had his hair cut in a short back and sides. But we never reached the elusive First Day of Principal Photography.

In the company of my downcast crew, I stood on a hilltop at our remote farmhouse location and loudly cursed the heavens. The celestial response was to cause the sun to shine, unabated, for the duration of what would have been our whole shooting schedule. The script had demanded a heatwave and here it was now, frustratingly hot.

The gods were saying a final 'fuck you and your precious film-making'.

It was my own personal fall in France.

George Martin's film career was not to be. Mine was on the skids.

'Worse than the music business,' he said to me, after the debacle was complete and I was back at his rectory house in England. Even so, George mixed me one of his signature gin martinis. That was the measure of the man.

Sir George Martin, often referred to as 'the fifth Beatle' (although never by himself), wrote three books about his life and experience in that same music business. Now his manager, Adam Sharp, was calling me, wanting to know if I would be interested in combining, editing and curating all three volumes into one, with the aim of producing the definitive George Martin autobiography. He said that the Martin family wanted a writer who had personally known George to undertake the task.

I didn't bother to feign the slightest disinterest, not even for comic effect.

I just started to drive more slowly.

MONDAY, 25 APRIL 2016

I am back in The Hospital after our weekend of torment.

Dr Juliette Sheridan apologises profusely for her colleague's intervention the previous Friday. Juliette is so kind, warm and caring to Deirdre and myself that we are able to move on from that event.

She confirms, knowing it will come as no surprise, that as well as the primary bowel cancer, the liver biopsy results have shown a very large secondary tumour. The crucial question is whether there is a chance of performing successful surgery on such a beast. If there isn't, then the prognosis will be very tough. There is only one man who can answer that question. And Justin Geoghegan is soon with us. He sits down quietly in a chair, as more golfers tee off outside. Dr Geoghegan chooses his words carefully and, to my mind, exquisitely.

Yes, he says, he thinks that he will be able to perform the surgery to remove the secondary cancer. The procedure is called a liver 'resection'. The tumour is unusually large, but it is still technically 'resectable', meaning that it can be extracted by skill and scalpel. The word becomes my immediate mantra: resectable, resectable, resectable. (In due course, I also get used to enthusiastically employing one of life's greatest clichés: that there is light at the end of the tunnel.)

Justin will attempt to remove the tumour and about half of the liver itself. He plans to leave as large a margin as possible between the remaining 'good' tissue and the blighted part which has been affected by the cancer and must be excised. Another positive, Justin explains, is that the veins and arteries attaching this vital organ to other sections of the digestive system appear to be intact and useful. I am lucky, he says, because this isn't always the case. Amazingly, once the tumour and the 'bad' half of the liver have been removed, the remainder will grow back to full size within months. It's the only organ in the body to perform this feat of self-renewal.

Normally chemotherapy would be employed to shrink or suspend the growth of a tumour before surgery. We are, Justin concludes, much too late for that.

His main surgery day is Thursday and he schedules me for the following week. The only reason I might have to wait longer than that is if an emergency liver transplant operation comes in, though he assures me that is a rare event.

We are firmly on the roller coaster now. In quick succession I meet the rest of my consultants and their supporting medical team. Dr Sean Martin, colorectal surgeon, an intriguing and charismatic young Tipperary man, is precise but also encouraging in his explanations. He tells me that an immediate priority is the placement of a metal stent into the lower reaches of my colon, in order to keep my digestive tract open. However, I will have to wait until tomorrow for the pleasure of that experience.

My oncologist, Dr David Fennelly, arrives next. He is tall and tanned, with an open smile. I am on my own in the hospital room, tired and not at my best. But I am uplifted when he says with optimism that I am an 'unusual' case. 'That's because I'm an unusual person,' I declare ridiculously, trying to match his upbeat tone. I cringe, but Dr Fennelly isn't remotely fazed. Oncologists have surely experienced every possible psychological response from their patients.

He continues with a definition of 'unusual'. After listening to David's words I conclude that in the grand scheme of things I should probably be riddled with cancer but, according to the initial CT scan and a subsequent, more detailed magnetic resonance imaging (MRI) scan of my whole body, I don't yet appear to be so. The two dangerously advanced sites are, perhaps, miraculously self-contained. David tells me that in his estimation my primary tumour in the colon probably started growing a year and a half ago, because the secondary liver metastasis is now so big. Too late for chemotherapy, he reiterates. Too late for anything but radical surgery. Then he says the only thing that I need to hear in this life.

'We view this as a very serious but curative situation, Stephen.'

I pause.

I look Dr Fennelly directly in the eyes. I feel my fear fall away.

'Do you really think that I can find a way through this?'

He smiles back at me.

'Yes. We do.'

The next day, completing the team (and making sure to get the professional titles correct here) I meet the colorectal cancer nurse coordinator, Anne White. A breeze of fresh, spiritually restorative, intoxicating air would have the same effect as Anne does on entering a room. A music-loving, immensely attractive person with a mischievous sense of humour, Anne's role is to keep me completely informed of the medical team's plans and smooth the bumpy journey as best she can. She's brilliant at the task, and over the coming months and years I rely on her unashamedly, through all her caring explanations, through all my trepidations and occasional tears.

***

Deirdre and I start to navigate the ten days before the liver surgery. It seems like a long time, particularly when there is little to do but think. It is not the body that panics. It is the mind. On the medical side we have decided to trust our team completely. They have already given us that confidence and we intend to treasure it. In that context, I have decided to stay away from Internet searches, where potentially comforting knowledge would inevitably intermingle with car-crash case studies.

But on the mental side and the spiritual side, I am not best prepared for this fight. Having spent my life up to now sliding between agnosticism, a rejection of religious instruction, with a strong sense of my own hubris when life has gone well, and a failure to engage with any spiritual explorations or beliefs when it hasn't, I am now left in a vulnerable place.

It is a difficult thought process to convey. We have all read and heard of this drastic moment when you are suddenly facing the real possibility of death. And it is not feasible to deny the sense of the surreal when it actually happens.

However, if there is one change in my thought process that I can report from this period, it is simply this: that every person, place and event that I encounter (with all five of my senses) is more interesting and affecting than ever before.

I also find myself looking back into my own history for moments that I can weigh down with importance. I study the patterns, coincidences, links and stories in my life, of which there have been many. I want to believe that there are reasons why various people have crossed my path, reasons why I am drawn to particular places, and reasons why events have taken place and will occur in the future. At times that search fills me with joy, moments of sharp consciousness, or tremors of unhappiness.

Here in my alien room, at the far reaches of The Hospital,

a hot sun burns through the windows onto my bed, as I mull over flashes of the past. For some reason, I think of the famous polemicist, Christopher Hitchens, proudly and consistently atheistic to the end of his own journey with cancer. My mind then takes me to the other end of the scale, to the people who are convinced that spiritual and religious miracles alone have been their cure.

I also remember various occasions when I accompanied my much-loved and terminally ill eldest sister, Fiona, as she sought some spiritual equilibrium. I recall her particular dis-illusionment after meeting a Buddhist rinpoche who had been unable to provide the wise counsel that she felt she needed. Fiona died from secondary breast cancer in 2002, at the age of forty-one, after an all-too-brief but shining career as a medical doctor committed to working with those on the so-called margins of society, as well as considerable achievements in the spheres of political, educational and social activism. At the very end, despite the inexplicable injustice of her plight, I hoped that Fiona had found some peace for herself.

I know for certain that, wherever I settle in my mind, I have to engage with this arena of belief or non-belief. I don't have a choice. No one does. Because that state of inquisitive flux is inevitably stirred up in the shocked and addled psyche when your own potential demise comes into view.

Deirdre also lends me her own vitality and the benefit of her years of spiritual exploration: from conventional Christianity, to mindfulness, to positive thinking, to simple prayer or meditation, to discussions of world religions, to her basic idea that we humans are not designed to, or more importantly, that we are simply not able to, deal with this life and death without engaging our sense of the spiritual. Deirdre's heartfelt determinations are two-fold: firstly, that I will be cured and survive; and secondly, that in order to do so, I will need to find a way to believe it myself. That part is up to me.

***

The days before surgery pass slowly. I have to call my other sister, Suzie, who has flown to Croatia for a short break with her future husband, Pete. Of course, I am acutely aware that it is a case of déjà vu for her. She and I had the same telephone conversation with Fiona when she was first diagnosed. I try to reassure Suzie that, in spite of the fact that my case is serious, I will be fine in the end; that the doctors have emphasised how much cancer treatment has progressed in recent years, and how it is certainly a lot more advanced than in Fiona's time. I am dreading the same call to our parents, Pamela and Brendan. Suzie calmly advises me to tell it to them straight.

Pamela answers the phone. She is as strong and loving as ever, a recent cancer survivor herself, steamrollering over the news with optimistic chatter and life stories. Eighty-one now and a child of the Second World War, Pamela travelled on an overcrowded troopship from Bombay in Colonial India to Glasgow in Scotland when she was ten years old. She was in the company of her mother, Rosamond, and five-year-old brother, Richard. Her father, Cecil Coldicott, a major in the 6th Gurkha Rifles, had died of stomach cancer three years previously. Shortly after they arrived in Britain, Pamela and Richard were sent off to boarding school in England. Pamela comes from a different, more resilient generation than I do. But everyone is soft inside, never more than when their offspring are vulnerable. I wish that I could protect my mother from this news, rather than listening to her comforting attempts to protect and reassure me.

Pamela tells Brendan my diagnosis when he gets home. He phones and asks if he can come to see me straight away. I wait anxiously for him to arrive.

There were extraordinary parallels in the early lives of both my parents: my father's mother, Sheila, also died of cancer, before Brendan had reached double digits. He too had been sent away to an English boarding school, near London. When he was summoned home he thought that it was for safety reasons, because German V1 'doodlebug' bombs were falling on and around that city. He arrived back in Dublin to find his mother inexplicably bed-bound and he was immediately sent away again, to a nearby boarding school in Clontarf. A month later, Brendan was the last pupil to be collected at the end of term. His father, Herbert, eventually picked him up in a pony and trap. As they trotted down the long school driveway, Herbert told Brendan that his mother was dead.

During Fiona's illness, Dad had tried to move heaven and earth to fix her. As he arrives at The Hospital, I want to convince him that I am a different case, that there will be a different outcome. But some gap in communication means he hasn't yet realised that I already have the secondary diagnosis. His eyes well up. He finds it hard to accept the positive view that I subsequently try to push. He doesn't say so, of course, but I know that the pain of going through this again will take him to the edge. He also needs to find a way to believe in an optimistic end to this. No matter how much I wish it, I can't do it for him. I have to focus on myself.

That night, as the nurses settle me down with Xanax and sleeping tablets, the best I can do to cheer myself up is to murmur a version of the catchy Mel and Sue pop song containing the chorus lyrics: 'I'm never going to be respectable.' Who knows where it has come from, but it invades my personal space like a weird flashback. In my head I change the words to: 'I'm always going to be resectable.'

It's a start.

If an unavoidably demented one.

SEARCHING

After I had received the second draft of *The Safe*, and started some preliminary research for the George Martin book, the budding warmth of spring arrived. As they say in these parts, there was a grand stretch in the evenings. We readied ourselves to move into the newly renovated house and took our excited children to see it. Fortunately, and crucially, Holly and Daniel both chose the bedrooms we had allocated to them, and so peace was declared.

In general, I could feel my energy levels starting to soar. But I was still waiting for more opportunities and stars to align. In terms of the way this precarious creative enterprise works, I needed to get at least four or five additional horses into the race, for the odds to improve.

The next horse was, with a true sense of the absurd, literally a horse. I was sent a copy of a book called *Centaur*, to see if I would consider adapting it for the big screen, and to discover in turn whether I was the right person for the job. The cover of the paperback had a haunting image of a leaping racehorse, as if captured by a CT scan. The accompanying words were beguilingly simple:

A Man.

A Horse.

A Ghost.

I hadn't heard of this barely believable true story about a jockey's survival and rehabilitation following a shocking fall. In truth, I hadn't even ridden a horse myself. I only knew of their equine power and spirit because I had directed two documentaries set in the rarefied world of a champion jockey and an elite trainer. Before that I hadn't been interested in the sport. Now I was fascinated by it, and also a little knowledgeable, which is always a dangerous thing.

I met *Centaur*'s director to discuss the demands of a potential screenplay for this cleverly crafted autobiography. For the first time in a couple of years I was back in a realm I was comfortingly familiar with. I knew the often-clumsy vernacular of the process: should we adopt a non-linear structure? What supporting characters should we focus on? What parts of the book would have to be sacrificed?

We were looking for a visual storytelling device to help us deal with all of the following angles: the protagonist's near-death during a horse race; the bizarre fact that his father's fear of flying delayed the jockey's life-support machine being switched off, and that he had regained consciousness again by the time his dad arrived by ferry; the blissful few years with his beautiful girlfriend before the horrific fall; the memory loss which meant that he couldn't remember those blissful years; the fact that the jockey admitted this mental blank to no one, least of all his beautiful, loyal and supportive girlfriend (I did say clumsy vernacular); and, finally, his grinding but triumphant return to bodily strength, and to the winner's enclosure in a major race.

I loved the book. It was garnering awards and moving into the arena of hot property. There were a couple of further meetings, lunches and telephone discussions. I made my pitch and waited for an offer from the director, to see if this particular horse was going to join my race.

While I did so, another idea emerged from the ether. A decade ago, I met Jade Caswell. She was eighteen and had just signed a major British recording deal through her manager, Daniel Ryan, who had previously played in a successful Irish band called *The Thrills*. I filmed Jade as she wrote and recorded songs in Dublin, London and Los Angeles, with a coterie of high-flying producers. We had a lot of laughs. She was going to be the next big thing. Then her world fell apart. Politics and personnel changes at the record company stalled the progress of her album. There were wrangles over whether she had written a song that was commercial enough to justify a big release. Meanwhile, Jade was burning through her considerable advance with gusto. She told me that the eventual low point, after the drugs and the booze and the couch-surfing homelessness, was when she was falsely imprisoned and violently assaulted in an apartment in Portugal. She was convinced that she was going to die.

A decade later, I bumped into Jade again. She wasn't low any more. She was ready to rumble. But at the ripe old age of twenty-eight the music industry didn't want to know her because she had shown herself to be so terribly human in her failings. So much for rock 'n' roll. I still had hours and hours of the documentary footage we had shot ten years ago. There was also a short promotional clip from that time. The promo was a little saccharine-flavoured, because the prying eyes of the record company overlooked everything. But it did give a glimpse of Jade's story, amid the naive excitement before her troubles started. I began to wonder if the old footage could still be put to some interesting and valuable purpose all this time later.

Jade was a very different woman now. She was still young and vibrant, but with a depth of harsh life experience behind her. She had a regular job, even if it was a little too conventional for her liking, and she was enjoying the stability of a long-term relationship. But she still burned with creative ambition. She wanted to return to the fray. Jade put her new perspective to me in a couple of simple, powerful sentences: 'I didn't know who I was then. I do now.'

Even so, we both needed to be wary. I didn't want to be the one to knock her off course in a negative way, if that was a possibility. At the same time, it was stating the obvious to say that she was her own person now, and she didn't need me to patronise or paternalise her in any way.

When we met up again, over many cups of strong coffee, we had some very frank discussions on a range of topics. Many of them were about her mishaps and my illness. The sense of honesty we had with each other reflected the way it had always been between us in the distant past, and that was reassuring for us both.

We got down to the nitty-gritty. Jade was interested in acting and I was interested in working with her again. The thought crossed my mind that I could tell a fictional version of her story, with a character close enough to the reality but not an exact replication, weaving some of the old footage into what script editors like to call an 'inciting incident'. It would be a coming-of-age story as old as life itself, but a harsh, broken, beautiful one full to the brim with Jade's talent.

I approached a few of my favourite people to see if they would potentially collaborate with us. They all made positive noises. I prepared to describe it to the development financiers. Inevitably, at some stage, I would end up employing the usual naff shorthand:

Boyhood meets *Once*?

Then I hit the first bump on this particular development road.

'That's a musical,' my wife said to me, accurately and mischievously. 'You hate musicals.'

THURSDAY, 28 APRIL 2016

The day of my liver operation arrives.

I've been fasting since last night. Deirdre comes to The Hospital early and helps me to pack. After the surgery, I will be going into the Intensive Care Unit and then a post-operative ward, so we need to vacate my single room. I am as ready as I'll ever be and my lovely wife is keeping me calm. I hear the footsteps of a nurse coming to collect me and I also expect to see a hospital porter with a wheelchair, as is the norm. There's a knock and the door opens.

'I've been told to let you break your fast,' the nurse says flatly. 'I can get you some tea and toast if you like?'

Deirdre and I look at each other with a rueful smile. We know what this means. An emergency liver transplant must have come in. Bad luck for me, but life-saving good luck for someone else. In that context we can't complain. After ten minutes of disappointment, we rally our spirits and lie down on the bed for a comforting hug.

At mid-morning, we discover that two back-to-back emergency liver transplants are in progress, an event as rare as a blue moon. I am definitely off the surgical list for the day.

By coincidence, Deirdre meets Justin Geoghegan. He's at the coffee dock, taking a break between his two epic transplant operations. He graciously and unnecessarily apologises to Deirdre, emphasising the rarity of the occurrence.

We can only be philosophical about the delay, but it does feel like a blow. I will now need to wait another full week. During that time, I notice that I am consuming food and calories in large quantities, but they aren't destined for me. The tumours are robbing everything, even the extraordinarily calorific Fresubin drinks that I am introduced to for the first time. These little bottles of sickly sweet gunk will become part of my staple diet for the next year, helping to stem an alarming loss of weight. But I dread to think what my dentist is going to say when I next see him. For now, I am very thin, hungry and still shedding pounds. When I glimpse my body in the bathroom mirror, I am starting to look skeletal. The clock is definitely ticking.

The upside of the hiatus is that Juliette Sheridan continues to treat me with intravenous antibiotics, as well as other medical magic, and I continue to feel better in myself, although I do find myself starting to resent the golfers, who are constantly putting so badly on the green below my window. I envy their freedom and the banality of their game.

Thankfully Pamela, Brendan and Suzie are able and willing to visit me often. However, with frustrating timing for all concerned, their visits can be guaranteed to coincide with the arrival of a dietician, or a prepping anaesthetist, or a phlebotomist out looking for my blood, and the flow of most of our conversations is disrupted. Stephen Rennicks and my sister-in-law, Liz O'Kane, fill the late evening shifts when Deirdre is at home looking after our children. Then comes my moonlit ritual of pestering the night nurses for sleeping tablets or Xanax, and pulling the covers over my head in the darkness. Sometimes, last thing before I conk out, I watch documentaries on Netflix. In one of them, I see the iconic American writer Gore Vidal leaving his idyllic Italian cliff-top house on the Amalfi coast for the final time, after forty years of calling it his home. The melancholy is wrenching and tangible.

I don't want to leave my idyllic life. Inevitably, my mind also makes its own visits: to the imminent possibility of ending my days in a hospice if my medical path doesn't run smoothly; to all the regrets of the past, both personal and professional; to worries about money, bad investments and neglected insurance policies; to vast thoughts about my beloved wife and young children and how much quality time I will ever spend with them again; to a difficult acceptance that these events are all *really* happening and that there aren't any definite whys or wherefores.

During this week-long state of suspension, other moments of succour come in the form of visits by my ex-housemates Ed Guiney and Paul Hickey. They arrive to see me on separate occasions, both of them shifting busy family, film-making and acting schedules to get here. We had spent so many exciting and memorable days and nights together as young bachelors, assuming that life would never change. Now, much later in our lives, there's a man overboard. It's all hands on deck.

Ed and I go back a long way, to the mid-1980s. We used to meet haphazardly at college parties, inevitably ending up discussing actors, films and hazy ambitions for the future. After we started Temple Films in 1992, there were a quick-fire few years during which we worked together on the debut films of five directors, myself included. It was a hectic and generally enjoyable learning curve. In retrospect, they were rose-hued, carefree and happy days. A little later, Ed agreed to be my best man when Deirdre and I got married during a Halloween storm, in the Gothic revival surroundings of Kinnitty Castle. As we had been a couple for quite some time at that stage, my wife accurately described it as 'the seven year hitch'. The wedding took place in 2000, which simplifies the otherwise complicated and potentially treacherous mathematics involved in getting each anniversary right.

Now, sixteen years later, Ed and I sit together unexpectedly, here in The Hospital. I welcome the distraction of our chat about recent events in his career, Ed having just produced the Oscar-winning *Room*, with more exciting projects on the horizon. He wouldn't be the boasting type, however. You'd have to pull the detail out of him. But I'm quite good at that, particularly when it comes to juicy film anecdotes. I love to hear tales of the highs and lows behind every production. In the silent simplicity that exists between long-standing friends, we don't need to talk too much about the details of my medical predicament. Ed's parents were both eminent doctors and his brother still is. It is left unsaid between us, but Ed knows that I have a good old fight on my hands.

Paul Hickey and I have been friends for almost as long. After our bachelor pad with Ed broke up (Deirdre lived next door and so that was the end of me), Paul took his acting skills to London and carved out a successful career in theatre, television and voice-over. When Deirdre and I eventually followed him, we ended up living very close to Paul and his wife, Becky. As ten busy London years flew by, our kids grew up together and post-Sunday-lunch afternoons were full of wine-fuelled debates and high laughs. Paul has now returned to the auld sod to visit me in less happy times. I hugely appreciate him making the journey and bringing me back those sweet memories.

The last of my callers, completing the small closed circle of people I invite to visit me, is Paki Smith. I first met him in 1987, when he designed the sets for a university theatre tour we went on together, travelling around the north-eastern seaboard of the United States of America. That ambitious tour was the brainchild of our mutual friend and producer, Richard Cook, who later became my agent and the founder of many successful adventures such as *The Cat Laughs Comedy Festival* and *Kilkenomics*.

Paki Smith and I were the only two in the group of sixteen students who had international driving licences. So we covered a lot of miles between us, in a rented U-Haul truck and a battered station wagon. In addition, the tour was just tough enough to cure me of my delusions about becoming a professional actor. (It also didn't help that I lacked the necessary physique, voice control or performing charisma.) It was time instead, I realised, to think about producing, writing or directing. Anything but treading the unforgiving boards.

Later, I dragged Paki from his painter's studio into the world of film production design. He worked on my first short, *Reaper,* and then co-designed *Sweety Barrett,* both of which were produced by Ed Guiney. Paki still designs exciting film productions across the globe, while continuing his career as a fine artist. Languishing in my sickbed, I can vicariously visit those new film sets through Paki's war stories. In The Hospital, our conversation takes us to every corner of life, often through Paki's sense of curiosity as a voracious reader. We also laugh regularly together, engaging in the Irish pastime known as 'talking bollocks'.

When I first met Paki in our early twenties, he was a declared Christian. All of his paintings were on religious themes. One I especially loved was an oil painting on a circular wooden board, of Christ with his wild hair going up in flames. Paki's not so fervently Christian now, he's more of a broad spiritual adventurer, but that painting is etched on my mind forever. I think he sold it to someone in Lake Placid, upstate New York. He mounted an exhibition there, after our student theatre tour had finished and we both went to work in a restaurant to pay off our debts. I envy that painting's owner. It was a veritable thing of beauty.

***

The hardest moments before the liver surgery are when I am alone and my mind is in free-fall. I listen to the radio and obsess over the stories and reports that I hear, as I try to figure out where I fit into them: two cancer survivors discuss the importance of diet for remission; there's an historical account about the residential square I have recently moved into, describing details about the murder of a suspected informer there a hundred years ago, during the Easter Rising of 1916; in current news, where I don't fit in at all, there's the failure of Irish politicians to form a government almost a hundred days after the general election.

Then, from Britain, comes the conclusion of the second Hillsborough inquest into the death of ninety-six football fans from Liverpool Football Club in April 1989. I listen intently to this radio report. The verdict at the inquest states that the fans were unlawfully killed due to the gross negligence of police during a crush in the crowd. It has taken the families of the deceased almost twenty years of struggle and campaigning to secure this conclusion.

The broadcast features a live link to a rally on the streets of Liverpool. I have followed the fortunes of that city's football club (the red one) for as long as I can remember, and now my young son does so as well. I also recently filmed large parts of *Noble* there. I can see the place vividly in my mind's eye. To hear the whole Hillsborough story again is suddenly and unexpectedly emotional for me in my present state.

Live on air, Kenny Dalglish, former star player and ex-manager of the football club, reads a poem called 'Footprints in the Sand' to a large Liverpool crowd. The narrator in the poem describes a dream in which she walks on a beach, side by side with Jesus. Their two sets of footprints run parallel behind them in the sand. As her past life flashes by in the dream, the narrator realises that, during all the hardest times, only one pair of footsteps remained. This is followed by her accusatory question to Jesus. Why did he desert her in those moments, just when she was most in need of his help? The poem ends with Jesus's gentle rebuke to his doubter: there was only one set of footprints in the sand during those tough times, he says, because he had picked her up and carried her. As I listen to this on the radio, I conjure the poem's final image clearly in my mind – the single-file tracks on the beach under a dark and oily sky – as if it is another Paki Smith oil painting.

After the poem, the whole crowd sings the Anfield anthem, 'You'll Never Walk Alone', in spine-tingling unison. Liverpool football supporters adopted that song after it became a popular hit, in a version recorded by local group Gerry and the Pacemakers. George Martin produced that chart-busting single, at Abbey Road, in 1963.

The night before my operation I meet Rose for the first time. She has been in the room next door to me for two weeks, but we hadn't set eyes on each other. A small, frail woman in her sixties, she is suffering from chronic breathing difficulties. She often wakes up in a panic in the middle of the night. She shouts out repeatedly for a nurse because she can't reach her call bell. Her weak voice never carries down the long corridor to the nurses' station. So I end up pressing my own button until attention arrives for Rose.

'I've been keeping you awake, Stephen,' she says with a big smile, when we finally meet outside the doors of our adjacent rooms. Rose thrusts a Mass card into my hand and wishes me good luck, clasping my wrist tightly. She looks earnestly into my eyes and her rattling, chesty voice is filled with compassion: 'I think you should read this before your operation tomorrow.' I thank Rose for her kindness, and we both retreat into our cubbyholes, like time-keeping figures on a German cuckoo clock. I read the prayer on the card. It suggests that I should accept my own suffering so that I can understand the suffering of Jesus. I'm not convinced. However, I do like the idea of being carried. I could use all the help I can get. Maybe you just can't have it both ways.

By now, I have had enough of the cabin fever and the

waiting. My head is too full of thoughts. Uncertainty can only be solved by action. Thankfully, early the next morning I am first up on the operating schedule. Juliette Sheridan and her team of junior doctors are there to wish me luck. So is Anne White, conscientiously making sure that everything goes to plan.

This part is the hardest for Deirdre, who now has to face the long wait for news. The whole team is there for her as well. We have all got to know each other by now, three weeks in. Because of their reassurance, I can relax a little and face forward into this process.

After I kiss my wife goodbye, I wait on my trolley in the pre-op area. Out of the corner of my eye, I see Justin Geoghegan entering a sealed area, to scrub up.

I'm on.

In an operating theatre with windows on three sides and bright spring sunshine flooding in, a young anaesthetist expertly sticks a needle into my lower back. As loud classical music plays on the stereo (yes, it really is like in the movies), I lie down for an oxygen mask and the other sedatives that are needed to take me where I am going.

I'm ready.

I have to be.

.

.

.

.

FAILING

As 2018 progressed, I was grateful for the creative opportunities that arose, particularly as they seemed to be accompanied by a physical and mental energy to match them. For a long time, I had worried that I would never experience that sense of excitement and satisfaction again.

When I was diagnosed with cancer I had to abandon much. Throughout my treatment the world shrank and became flat. I had no option other than to leave some people and plans in my wake.

As I tried to avoid another type of wake.

Instead of being in my sickbed, I should have been out hustling. I had already spent a long time promoting and publicising *Noble*, mainly in America and back home in Ireland. Unlike the vacant aftermath of the Burgundy experience, this time I had the chance of opening some doors. Both the film and its cast had won festival awards, and reviewers had responded well to the cinematic telling of Christina Noble's story. She was played, at different ages and stages of her life, by three actresses, each perfectly matched in appearance and talent: Deirdre O'Kane, Sarah Greene and Gloria Cramer

Curtis. The acting line-up also included Brendan Coyle, Liam Cunningham and Ruth Negga, each bolstering the media's interest in the film. (It's a must-see, obviously!)

After we completed post-production, the expectation for wide and prominent distribution was high. I might say unrealistically high, except for the fact that there were a couple of occasions when the film could have had genuine lift-off, flirting with large international marketing and distribution deals only for that possibility to drift agonisingly away again. Instead, it took the middle road. Which is not such a bad road, in a world that produces about ten thousand films a year. From my own personal and professional point of view, if I had not been waylaid by illness, *Noble* would have given me the chance to engage with interesting producers, writers and actors, leading to a healthy range of opportunities for development and production. To an extent, it still does give me that prospect, as films now have such long and accessible lives. With the proliferation of distribution platforms on the Internet, titles can be found by audiences for many years after their initial release. But there is no doubt that, as a result of my cancer, I missed out on much of the momentum that the film afforded me.

There were other sad professional farewells. A US television network based in London had commissioned me to develop a drama from a family memoir for which they had purchased the adaptation rights. It was an intriguing story about members of a British dynasty who made their fortune dealing in African ostrich feathers during the late nineteenth century. Traders at the time were convinced that the fashionable accoutrements would prove as valuable a long-term investment as gold and diamonds. Inevitably, in this true story of a classic economic bubble, both the feathers and the family crashed and burned. Unfortunately, so had I.

Before that I had been chatting about, workshopping and attempting to write a heist film with a difference. The difference being that I was co-creating it with five of my favourite actors. They had become a gang of friends when I cast them together in my comedy-horror *Boy Eats Girl* (2005) and their close camaraderie had lasted over the intervening decade. Their careers had generally flourished and one of them had become a bona fide, brightly burning film star. Everything was apparently there for me on a plate. But I struggled and struggled to make the heist screenplay work. My floundering efforts on it were frustratingly substandard over an eighteen-month period up to the diagnosis of my cancer.

Later, I remembered that my oncologist had talked about the length of time that he thought my tumours had been growing, considering their stage and size.

'About eighteen months,' he had estimated.

At least now I had an excuse.

But did I also have an excuse for not returning to the script after my treatment was over? I was terrified of failing again and of failing the actors again. The development-financing executive for this potential project sympathised and said that she had been through a similar predicament in her own writing days. She kindly told me that she would understand my decision, if I couldn't face re-entering that space, which held such dark associations and feelings of inadequacy.

I couldn't.

And in the end I didn't need to. Another heist film with a very similar premise was already being made. It was my coward's way out.

But the five actors still loved me.

And I loved them back.

THURSDAY, 5 MAY 2016

I wake up in the Intensive Care Unit after my liver resection.

Deirdre's beautiful face is smiling at me, both relieved and reassuring. I mispronounce some garbled nonsense and fall back to sleep.

Justin Geoghegan pays me a visit to report on his handiwork. 'I don't know how much you'll remember of this conversation,' he says gently, 'but it all went well, all went to plan.'

'Were you happy with the margins?' I ask through the stupor, remembering enough from my former life to know that margins are important.

'I was. Yes,' he grins, satisfyingly.

If he is happy, then I am happy. I settle into the surreal, blue-lit gloom of the ICU under the very intense care of my one-on-one nurse, Adrian, who, I discover, is Welsh, though I don't hold that against him. He works hard all through the night, as I drift between sleep and unhinged wakefulness. Adrian operates inflatable pumps to massage my legs and prevent clotting. He empties several drains, bags and sumps and he even gives me a full body wash. I've never flown first class before. It's an impressive service.

Just after the witching hour and still quite out of it, I hear them coming. The cardiac team sets up shop at the end of my bed and readies the jump leads for electric shock re-starts. I put my hand to my chest and feel the ridiculously high rate of my heartbeat. No wonder they are worried. I can hear them whispering and conspiring against me, as they speak urgently to the pain management nurse, who seems to be permanently stationed at a school desk in the middle of the room. Then, boom! They part the metal double doors and disappear into an adjoining ward with all their equipment. They weren't here for me after all. Some other poor unfortunate next door has real heart problems. My selfish relief is palpable.

Next, a load of very drunk men arrive, speaking loudly in an unknown language. They must be on the way back from the pub, I speculate to myself. The intruders seem to be wheeling another patient on a trolley. Nurse Adrian does his best to shush them, gesturing towards my outstretched body. Eventually they leave, singing an unknown melody.

I hear a voice in my head.

'It's a strange world, isn't it?'

Blue Velvet (dir. David Lynch, 1986).

***

By the time I am moved onto St Luke's ward the next day, I am much more compos mentis. But now the pain is kicking in. As well as a narrow-gauged tube that travels under my skin and around the site of the surgery delivering morphine, I am also entitled to a patient-controlled analgesia pump (PCA). This is a sophisticated piece of kit, clamped to the edge of my bed, which allows me to administer an additional dose of morphine by pressing a button. The pain-relieving liquid then passes through a cannula tube inserted straight into a vein in my arm. I can administer this morphine every ten minutes, if I wish, and the pump is strictly regulated to prevent overdose. Giving patients control of their own post-operative pain is surely one of the wonders of modern medical science.

I'm less in awe of modern medical practices, however, when a physiotherapist arrives and expects me to stand up, before transferring to a chair by the bed. I remember from my wife's experience, after the births of our children by Caesarean section, that this enforced mobility following surgery is *de rigueur* nowadays. In my case, I have ten tubes or drainage bags attached, and it takes the physiotherapist twenty minutes to position them all for the space walk. I'm pressing the PCA to beat the band and eventually I make it to the chair, two feet away.

Then disaster strikes.

Deirdre is performing her latest stand-up comedy show, *1DEE*, at Vicar Street Theatre tomorrow night, in front of a thousand paying punters. She has lost the only copy of her script, complete with hand-written additions. My wife arrives on the ward genuinely distraught. It's the stagecraft equivalent of someone pulling all my tubes out.

I try to calm her down. I tell her that she has performed the show many times and knows it backwards. My logic falls on deaf comedian ears. There's no comfort to be found here on St Luke's ward, so I send Deirdre home to keep searching for the manuscript. I feel desperately sorry for her. It's a stress that she doesn't need on top of all of this, and I can see that the pressure of such a hugely important show, booked many months in advance of my diagnosis, is almost too much for her to bear.

As if the missing 'comedy bible' isn't enough, I realise that I am now starting to hallucinate. Everything I look at is beginning to move strangely, alter its state, or strobe. Alarm bells ring in my head. At the time that my sister Fiona was diagnosed with her secondary cancer, we were told that it might affect her brain function. Then one day, when Fiona started asking us if we could see a small creature standing in her doorway, we assumed that it was the onset of the threatened degeneration. It wasn't. It was only the morphine talking and, once it was successfully calibrated, she ended up being very lucid for her remaining two years of enthusiastic living.

My morphine side effects are a pale imitation of Fiona's, but I know that, if they aren't dealt with, they will get worse. To make matters even more urgent, it is Friday afternoon. The previously mentioned skeleton crew of nurses and reduced dose of doctors is about to come into being once more. I start kicking up a fuss, working against the clock. Elaine, my pain management nurse, does the business for me by collaring a consultant anaesthetist just as he exits an operating theatre, and before he has a chance to call it a weekend. Dr Hugh Gallagher arrives with a sense of humour and willingness for action. He says that I am obviously allergic to the natural morphine I am receiving and that I need to be switched to the synthetic variety. I am quickly saved from a couple of days of horrible drug-induced imaginings.

Even better, I receive a text from Deirdre.

Found it!

I can breathe easy again.

***

Early on Saturday morning, flatly contradicting my previous contention about the dearth of medics at weekends, Justin Geoghegan comes to check up on me. So do Juliette Sheridan and her posse of junior doctors, followed by anaesthetist Dr Hugh Gallagher. And I'm not even his patient. Sometimes you just have to admit to being spoilt.

Although, that's not always the way I feel with my five fellow inpatients. Needless to say, the dynamics of a ward have a major impact on you as you struggle to get well. Now a new inhabitant arrives, with swollen red legs and no stated diagnosis. He never stops talking and I'm too ill to enjoy the banter. He endears himself to me even less when I am wheeled out for a chest X-ray and he says: 'You look very grey!' On my return, and again too enthusiastically for my liking, Red Legs adds: 'I really didn't think you were going to make it there, pal!'

My next-door neighbours are chalk and cheese. On my right is a forty-year-old with a case of diverticulitis that has already been successfully treated. He's waiting for doctors to conduct his final case review. Until then, his visiting teenage sons and daughters are keeping him entertained, and he makes business calls on a mobile phone. On my left is an octogenarian man who has suddenly decided that his time is up. He has concluded that an accident he had with some garden fertiliser a couple of years ago, and which has nothing to do with his diagnosed gall-bladder problems, has mysteriously done him in. He gathers his family to tell them of his decision to ask for a hospice place and to face his imminent death with dignity. All of this happens a yard away from me, on the other side of a stripy curtain like something from a children's puppet theatre.

But Red-Legged Big Talker is having none of it, and when the doctors come on their rounds, he turns informer on the old man and tells them of his fatal fertiliser self-diagnosis. The poor geriatric patient is reassured that his medical problems are not nearly as serious as he thought they were, and have nothing to do with garden phosphates. He has to call his family back again to break the good news. They reassemble the next day, just beyond the flimsy partition of my circus curtain. One relative, on hearing of the old man's reprieve, shouts at him with tearful relief: 'Don't you ever fecking do that to me again!' It's a ward-stopping moment.

The next day an Eastern European man with a stab wound appears on our ward, after life-saving surgery by 'Gold Fingers' Geoghegan. The new patient begins long and very passionate telephone conversations in his native language, sometimes annoyingly late into the night and after 'lights out'.

'I think if we could understand him,' Diverticulitis pipes up, 'we'd probably find out that there's more to this case than meets the eye.' He's not wrong. A woman who appears to be the injured man's wife arrives and leaves just as quickly, amid tears and raised voices. The next day someone different comes in to apparently stake her claim during visitors' hours.

'What did I tell you about his stabbing?' Diverticulitis whispers to me loudly and with great satisfaction. 'It was a crime of passion!'

With that, Diverticulitis takes his leave. Cured, reinvigorated and smug. For all I know he is off to see Deirdre O'Kane performing stand-up comedy in Vicar Street, along with the other nine hundred and ninety-nine audience members. How she is literally keeping the show on the road, and also looking after our children on top of it all, I'm not quite sure.

By every account Deirdre has one of the best, most brilliantly controlled and funniest shows of her comedy career, receiving a standing ovation. To say that I am amazed and proud of her resilience is an understatement. As for me, I'm on the mend. Or, as my wife says when she tells her audience an unflattering, but not necessarily true, joke about me (which she regularly does):

'Don't be worrying about my husband. He gets half of every laugh I get.'

RECORDING

We met up at the pre-arranged landmark in the middle of Dublin city and I decided that, rather than sitting down in a formal setting, we would grab takeaway coffees and wander through the streets, until we found a place where it felt right for us to stall. That perambulation would get the small talk out of the way as well.

This was the first time that Jade Caswell and Toni O'Rourke had met each other, and the director in me was already directing proceedings. First impressions, that initial chemistry between the two young performers, was important, even before the concept was fully formed or a page of script was written. We eventually stopped in St Stephen's Green and sat down on a grassy bank in sunshine. There was just enough heat for us to get lost in our conversation, without being distracted by the world around us or the people kicking through the leaves as they passed us by.

I was starting to have strong ideas for this film, inspired by Jade's life story so far and the documentary footage that we had filmed together ten years previously. In contrast to my last production, *Noble*, I wanted to make this something low-key: small cast, minimal budget, intimate and unusual. Possibly shooting on a compact digital camera, with a crew of only six or eight. A little 'film family' at work. If I could achieve those things, I could perhaps realistically be shooting it within eighteen months, a wet week in film development terms, but the kind of time frame that I needed to be driving towards with my new perception on life.

I had cast Toni O'Rourke in a small part in *Noble*, when she was still in her late teens. She initially flew out to Vietnam to look after Holly (seven) and Daniel (four) for us, during the long days when we were shooting Deirdre's scenes in the searing heat of Saigon. I knew that Toni had already featured briefly in a couple of productions, with directors I trusted. So I had no fear of casting her in a tiny but pivotal role that was to be filmed in the depths of winter, on the other side of the world, in Liverpool. However, the rest of my large film crew didn't know that. They thought that the director had lost the plot. I could hear mutterings and sniggers, as the rumours went around that I had gone and cast our childminder. The same one they had seen at the hotel pool in Ho Chi Minh City, or clinging on to Holly and Daniel as she occasionally brought them to visit the set. That misapprehension placed extra pressure on Toni. Then, when it came to her moment, over two or three shooting days, she put everyone in their place with a strong performance, acting up against the powerhouse duo of Sarah Greene and Ruth Negga. In the parlance, she nailed it.

Since then, Toni had trained at The Gaiety School of Acting in Dublin and been cast in several successful films and plays. She's on her way to a potentially exciting career (nothing in this business is definite, as Toni well knows) and it has been a pleasure to watch her upward trajectory. I did say little 'film family'. She's Deirdre's god-daughter. I've known her since she was a kid. Her boyfriend has agreed to produce this film with me and to play a part in it (he's a professional actor, don't worry). Her stepfather, my composer friend, Stephen Rennicks, was swiftly persuaded to oversee the music. His partner, the other Deirdre and my wife's best friend, was also going to be cast in the film, although she didn't know it yet. At that very moment in time, in the development of one project, at least, I needed to bring some of that familiarity (and talent) into my creative life.

Sitting there on the grass in St Stephen's Green, I asked Jade to tell Toni her story: all about the attempts to make it as a singer-songwriter at a very young age; descriptions of her travels and tribulations; memories of the events in her own personal tale of boom and bust. I also needed to hear it in Jade's own words again. The painful, private details contained in parts of the story weren't mine to reveal. Jade isn't as prissy as me. She was well able to pour out the narrative in all its complex colour. We had an immediate sense of trust, she and I, and she's happy to transfer that to anyone I put in front of her.

Jade and Toni. Toni and Jade. They just clicked. At a later meeting, I held out a bag full of the small high-definition videotapes, thirty or so in all, that I had filmed the documentary footage on all those years ago. After the two twenty-somethings had got over their laughter at the fact that I was still in possession of a video format which, as far as they were concerned, belonged in a museum, we managed to dip into the old images. The very first tape that Jade plucked out of the bag showed pictures of her much younger self, in an upscale London studio, recording a track she had written herself. Tears brimmed up in her eyes. She told us that song had been her favourite.

MONDAY, 10 MAY 2016

It's always hard to be allowed out of hospital after major surgery.

Your daily blood samples have to be saying the right things to the medics. The drains for your various fluids, including your urinary catheter, must function within an appropriate range. Your food, and the digestion of it, is closely monitored. It also doesn't help your cause if, like me, you are having nightly temperature spikes, which result in you needing to be hooked up to intravenous antibiotics in the early hours. Swabs of my nether regions reveal that I have contracted one of the hospital superbugs, called vancomycin-resistant enterococci (VRE). As far as I can gather, this means that I will be more susceptible to kidney, blood and other infections during the forthcoming chemotherapy. These conditions would have to be treated with antibiotics other than vancomycin, to which the bug is resistant, as the name suggests. VRE doesn't seem to have any immediately alarming symptoms, or worries in terms of passing on the infection when I eventually return home to my family. But in the meantime it does require segregation to a small ward of fellow VRE travellers.

One of my new companions is a gregarious French chef who has unluckily been re-admitted to hospital with fresh liver tumours shortly before his five-year remission anniversary. It seems cruel, but he shrugs it off. He advises the consumption of beetroot juice and eats from lavish cheese boards at his bedside table. Women call him constantly on the phone and he reassures them in high spirits, describing all the life adventures he is still destined to undertake. 'You have a lot of female fans,' I say, a little enviously. 'Oh, they love the gays!' he replies with Gallic flair. My 'gaydar' has let me down and I am strangely annoyed, trying pathetically as I am to be master of all I survey. French Chef laughs at me without animosity, and he tucks into another wheel of Camembert.

On the other side of the VRE room is a really tough case. A European ambassador to Ireland, once powerful, erudite and full of magnificent speech. He fell down the embassy stairs and has been reduced to an apparently vegetative state with total paralysis. But he is not alone in his plight. His attentive and courageous wife attends to him all day long and swears that he is slowly improving. She is joined by private agency nurses, whom she has hired to help her, usually a different one every day. They all ask the same list of questions about the ambassador's heart-rending story. Each day his wife repeats the same answers at length. It is clear that the process is therapeutic for her but, for French Chef and me, it's like a time warp. We find it very difficult to maintain a sense of humour amid the repetition. It reminds me of a Samuel Beckett play on a loop, and I curse my lack of patience and compassion. Thick waxy earplugs and distracting music from an iPhone become my close friends, day and night.

My main surgical wound is healing well. It's a fine-looking slice, from my sternum to my tummy button, with a sharp right-angle turn all the way across the bottom of my ribs. The large secondary tumour and the damaged half of my liver have been dispatched out of this hatch, and I am eternally grateful for that.

My small circle of visitors maintain a vigil. Gradually, the medical paraphernalia is stripped away. Eleven days after the operation, I am left with only one fluid drain, as a going home present. It is called a Hollister bag. For a few more days, it will draw and collect liquids from the site of the surgery and I will have to monitor its progress, up close and personal. I will need to keep a record of the flow in centilitres and phone my reports in to The Hospital.

My hero of the hour, Justin Geoghegan, gives me the go-ahead. I walk very gingerly towards the exit. Suzie picks up prescriptions for all kinds of maintenance drugs and painkillers on the way out. Driving home, we stop at my local pharmacy to acquire the medications. I begin a reluctant but very friendly acquaintance with the staff there. They will see a lot of me over the coming years.

When I get home, I settle into the comfort of our ridiculously large old bedroom, in the newly rented house. It wasn't originally intended for these serious bouts of convalescence, but it's going to have to serve the purpose and then some. Bizarrely, we haven't been able to move our own bed into the room because it is already possessed of a wooden four-poster, and that is beyond heavy. It reminds me, although unfortunately not for similar reasons, of our bridal suite in Kinnitty Castle during that memorable Halloween storm, some sixteen years ago. The wind whistles in through the gaps in the wooden window frames just to underline the comparison.

Ensconced in the bed, I immediately panic that I have been sent away from The Hospital without any antibiotics among my stack of medication from the pharmacy. I definitely don't want an infection to set me back. I telephone the nurses on St Luke's ward, to check whether this oversight is in error or not. I haven't meant for them to do this, but they call Justin Geoghegan at home, to enquire on my behalf, before getting back to me. I am told that no more antibiotics are required, and also that Dr Geoghegan says, if I need anything else, not to forget that he lives three doors away. Absurd serendipity.

My next task is to get going with chemotherapy as soon as is post-operatively possible. This is a vital stage. Not only do I have a primary colon tumour still in situ, but my medical team are also anxious to contain any stray cancer cells that may have been stirred up or released by the liver surgery. These could now be on the rampage, looking to set up base camp somewhere else in the body. There is also the issue of keeping the miraculous regrowth of the liver free of fresh tumours. No small concern.

Six weeks of convalescence need to pass before I can begin the chemo. During this period, I visit The Hospital again to have a minor surgical procedure. This is the insertion of a portacath, close to my right collarbone. The device, like a tiny drum, is positioned under the skin to provide permanent access to a vein. It will allow pre-medication and chemotherapy drugs to be introduced into my system every two weeks, through the most convenient, safe and easily repeatable method. It will also mean that I don't need to have a new puncture wound every time access to a vein is necessary. The portacath is a welcome relief from that ordeal. I have had so many injections, blood sample needles, and cannulas inserted by now that my veins have crept into hiding. Only the most expert doctors and nurses can find them and sometimes several sore attempts are necessary.

In the meantime, I have hit a wall of worry about pain relief. The pain manager at The Hospital has prescribed a fairly quick transition from opiates in tablet form (OxyContin and OxyNorm) towards over-the-counter ibuprofen. I understand the benefits of keeping medication to a minimum, particularly when I am already on quite a number of post-operative drugs and the Oxys can be addictive, but my head isn't in a happy place about the prospect of the proverbial aspirin or two.

I make an anxious visit to my original doctor's surgery. Ed McSwiney, who has emerged as my first saviour, for his insistence that I immediately attend The Hospital all those weeks ago, is on a day off. I have an appointment with one of his colleagues, Dr Claire Noonan, and her caring and concerned manner disarm me completely. The floodgates open for the very first time, as she lets me unburden and I cry like a small child. Claire understands every nuance of what I have been through and gives expression to a thought I haven't even solidified in myself: that I have been mentally toughing it out because I feel so protective towards my wife and children. She prescribes low doses of the same opiates to keep me going through the pain, both physical and psychological, and my equilibrium is largely and thankfully restored.

That is not to say that Deirdre and I don't continue to have a few more dark nights of the soul, lying in each other's arms. We do. But we also successfully divide the long journey ahead into manageable goals, to be scored one at a time. Deirdre's strength, and the support of my precious and carefully selected regular visitors, pull me through every time.

For many months, other members on both sides of my close family feel the strain also, of course. I was in that position myself when Fiona was ill, and I know it only too well. It's a feeling of helplessness and dread. A low-level anxiety floods your being and you dream of better days for all. There is a world of conversation, planning, suffering and comforting that the patient will never be a part of. This is not their place. This is the other side of the coping coin.

My mother, Pamela, has a horrific attack of vertigo, a weird and disabling dizziness and vomiting that is often brought on by stress. She is unable to speak because she's so ill; Brendan calls an ambulance for her and she is taken to The Hospital. For a while we are there together, on different wings.

Brendan is separately visiting wife and son.

Suzie is visiting mother and brother.

It must feel like a downward spiral.

But, as well as being sensitive souls, they are also tough as nails. They fight on through. Pamela eventually returns home. Nobody wants me to worry, so I'm not told much about the episode. They all conspire to keep me guilt free.

***

Responsibility for the next phase of my treatment moves to my oncologist, Dr David Fennelly. All the consultants will keep a watching brief, and my coordinating nurse, Anne White, will inform me of any updates in the medical team's thinking. I am aware that the regular private conferences, at which they discuss my case, result in the treatment being carefully tailored to it. There are other medical systems, used elsewhere in the world, that simply enter a patient into a protocol. They then receive the standard uniform treatment for their combination of symptoms and conditions. Not so here in The Hospital. Here, for each cancer patient, it's personal.

Deirdre comes with me to the first oncology appointment, to meet David Fennelly, and it's no bad thing for these two stars to align. My wife picks up on plenty of important detail that I miss, as he explains what lies ahead in calm, informative and reassuring words. It's another slightly surreal moment, even after major surgery, when you find yourself discussing the realities of your own chemotherapy treatment. The word itself carries such loaded connotations for all of us. But here I am now, talking to a medical expert for whom these discussions are a daily norm. In some odd way, I can embrace that. I really am a fully fledged cancer patient now.

I will be having six fortnightly sessions of a chemotherapy combination of drugs known as FOLFOX. Possible side effects are wide and varied but are usually confined to fatigue, dry and cracked skin, tingling numbness in fingers and toes, sore mouth and the disappearance of that most enjoyable of all the senses, taste. However, each individual responds to the chemicals differently, and I shall have to wait and see how my body behaves.

We ask Dr Fennelly what results we should hope for through this fairly short and sharp shock of treatment. He replies that he'd like to see the primary tumour in the colon shrink, the healthy regrowth of the liver without sign of damage or cancer and, obviously, the prevention of any possible further spread of the disease. But we all know that nothing is guaranteed. I marvel at his level-headed tone. He makes me feel that I am an important patient and not just a number in the ever-increasing twenty-first-century epidemic of cancer. I know from hearsay that David makes all of his other patients feel this way too, which must take an extraordinary amount of mental energy on his part.

Don't get me wrong. I am also a number: 0866248.

And my date of birth is 19-08-65.

I have to repeat all of those digits like a chant every time I undergo any medical procedure in The Hospital. They are also printed on my wristband and sometimes even on an ankle band. So far it has proved to be a successful basic security and identity check for the staff, which is the whole point.

'Now for the good stuff!' my oncology nurse announces loudly at my opening chemotherapy session. She is covered in protective clothing and a pair of eye goggles. In go the drips, hour after hour: antiemetics to prevent nausea, flushes and saline fluid to keep the veins clear, and finally the 'good stuff' itself: FOLFOX. ('Folfox sake!' I can't help my brain thinking.) It's dressed up in a garish purple bag to remind everyone that it is extremely poisonous and that spillage is to be avoided at all costs. As I lie childlike on the daybed, with my favourite blanket and pillow from home, the sac of liquid hangs on a metal stand over my head. I watch the chemical droplets descend slowly down their tube. I surrender to them.

It's undoubtedly a little counter-intuitive to allow your being to be flooded with toxicity, but I feel strangely grateful as the process begins. I am under no illusions about the serious nature of my prognosis. I haven't asked for the bookies' odds, the statistics, or the exceptions to the rule. There's absolutely no point. I have stayed true to my word, keeping away from reading about other patient case histories on the Internet. I have my own unique road to walk along, after all, and no one else has been down this very particular boreen before.

***

Paki Smith visits me at home after my first chemotherapy session. He presents me with a richly coloured and beautiful painting, oil on canvas, which he has just completed. Apparently, it's for me to keep. 'I was halfway through it when I realised it was you,' he says.

If that is the case, then it's a brave, somewhat abstract, version of Stephen Bradley. He's dressed as a top-hatted highwayman, brandishing a machine-gun in one hand, with the head of an axe in the other. Shooting and cutting. Behind me in the picture is that winding road I have to travel along, receding into the distance. Wherever it may take me, I am well-armed and ready. Paki has written the name of the painting on the back of the canvas: *The Fighting Man.*

I hang it up in pride of place.

I am on the road.

REMEMBERING

Now I was actually shooting again.

For the first time since I'd filmed a couple of live comedy gigs at the Everyman Theatre in Cork city three years previously, not realising that I was almost dead.

I was a Cork boy from the ages of six to twelve – my formative years perhaps – and I have always loved the place. When still only in his mid-thirties, Brendan had been appointed financial director of Youghal Carpets, and so our family made the move from Dublin. He and Pamela bought an unusually shaped, but beautiful, old house on the outskirts of the city, which they painted pale pink. They put goldfish in the pond, imported a donkey that foaled, and my mother had the idea of creating an organic fruit and vegetable shop, about thirty years ahead of her time. She grew kohlrabi and ornamental gourds in a field that had only ever known ancient forest, pasture or potatoes. Exotic avocados and fresh red chillies arrived ripe from Dublin on the train. My father built a large, plastic-sheeted, tubular hot house for cultivating tomatoes and lettuce. He bent the metal bars of the structure himself, with brute strength.

When Fiona and Suzie went to boarding school, I had the run of the place. At weekends, I would shuttle between my parents as they toiled away in the garden. I cunningly negotiated many a bilateral deal, resulting in a James Bond double bill at the Capitol Cinema on Grand Parade in the city centre, ostensibly as a reward for my parents' hard labour. Or, every May, I would force them to go to dinner at the posh Arbutus Lodge, so that I could watch the Eurovision Song Contest while they ate. It was revenge for the fact that – ridiculously, in my view – we didn't own a television set.

The county council decided to construct an enormous reservoir on a steep incline opposite our house, carving it out of the hillside with twenty mechanical diggers. From my bedroom window, my eight-year-old self saw the whole thing unfold, in glorious Technicolor, while I incessantly taped the top-forty music charts on my father's BASF reel-to-reel recorder.

Brendan pursued his lifelong passion for sailing, and we all spent long summer days, usually in the rain, exploring the beautiful local coastline from Kinsale to Crookhaven to Schull to Baltimore to Cape Clear and Sherkin islands.

At the five o'clock sunrise during the holidays, Fiona, Suzie and myself would cycle to our local farm and pick strawberries for a pittance a punnet.

One day, the police discovered and took away bars of gold that had been hidden in the middle of a wall near our pink house, remnants of a successful robbery some years previously.

When all of that excitement wasn't going on, I used to get the bus to secondary school at Midleton College, with my unrippable canvas schoolboy pass. On Saturdays, after the morning classes that some schools still inflicted back then, I was allowed to buy a bag of chips, with ketchup, for sixteen-and-a-half pence.

I thought that life would always be like that. Parts of it have been. Don't forget to enjoy the good times, people regularly remind us. Treasure each day, they urge. The past, and memories of it, play such a strong part in that process, putting everything in our lives into a personal context from which we can't escape. But moving forward isn't always as easy as we think it's going to be. Michael Finnegan, again.

Now, in the middle of 2018, I was finally on a studio set, shooting and directing once more.

I genuinely was remembering to enjoy it.

One of the prominent British television companies was interested in the idea of a comedy series with the working title of *The Deirdre O'Kane Show*. It commissioned a short pilot version, or 'taster'. In the wake of the *#MeToo* movement, the fairer sex were supposedly getting a fairer chance of being in the spotlight. Our comic mantra for the show was that women could say things now that men couldn't. We set up a writers' room and filmed four or five of the resulting sketches. In a nod to the work of the iconic Irish comedian, Dave Allen, these were intercut with Deirdre performing comic monologues seated in front of a very enthusiastic audience. They had been invited through her social media platforms, ensuring an excellent laughter track of hardcore fans.

We knew that the pilot wasn't for broadcast, so we had some fun toying with the commissioning editors and not worrying about the lawyers. Deirdre came up with the inspired character of a fictional agent, who represented not only Deirdre but also Harvey, Kevin, Woody, Roman, Louis and a whole list of 'fallen' men who were, if not quite imprisoned, at least presently unemployable. In the sketch the excitable agent character explained that, by default, Deirdre might finally get her own television show.

This playful conceit fitted Deirdre's agenda perfectly. As a woman who had broken through the glass ceiling of Irish comedy twenty years previously, she had long been awaiting some wry recompense for leading that particular struggle in such a male-dominated sphere. For my own part, I was just pleased to be shooting again, even if the production of the pilot was frustratingly limited in scope.

The initial response from the commissioning editors was encouragingly positive: they laughed.

Even though they were London-based, Barbara was Irish and Phil was Scottish, which was already a good start as far as our team was concerned. They had taken the bother to come to Dublin as we prepared to make the pilot. We also saw that as an expression of their enthusiasm, considering the heaviness of their respective workloads.

But commercial television in Britain is a tough nut to crack. The producers of the pilot had already been through a number of successful rounds of preliminary pitches before Deirdre and I had even become involved. There were complex corporate budgeting and scheduling structures that all commissions needed to fit into. Patience and perseverance were definitely called for and the decisions of the 'powers that be' at the broadcaster could not easily be predicted. There was also the danger of pushing too hard for an answer, provoking a negative response.

All we could realistically do now was hope and wait.

MONDAY, 11 JULY 2016

It is the second session of my chemotherapy that goes pear-shaped.

Ironically, it starts with an encouragingly positive development. Out of the blue, Dr Fennelly informs me that I have qualified for a relatively new immunotherapy drug, one of a group known as monoclonal antibodies. It's called Cetuximab and has the pharmaceutical trade name Erbitux. These treatments are sometimes also described as targeted therapies. My particular bowel cancer type possesses a large number of so-called receptors on the surface of the cells. When triggered, these allow the cancer cells to grow and divide. As far as I understand it, the Erbitux locks these receptors and inhibits such growth. Apparently there is also evidence that it may increase the effectiveness of the chemotherapy drugs. Only about a third of patients qualify for Erbitux. The tumour must have the RAS wild-type gene for it to work. Thankfully, I do have the wild-type gene. I also secretly like the name. It makes me think of *The Fighting Man*.

The nurses revel in telling me how expensive the drug is, as they hook me up for an extra two hours of intravenous flow, on top of my chemo. As it turns out, I am also lucky to have moved back to Ireland where, even as a public patient without insurance, I am entitled to receive this costly additional drug for free, because it is being paid for by the Health Service Executive (HSE). I am shocked to discover that, six months prior to my treatment, the NHS in England discontinued the deployment of Erbitux for patients with my condition. The National Institute for Health and Care Excellence (NICE) declared that purchasing the drug was not a cost-effective use of resources, even while recognising its substantial clinical benefits. The UK charity Beating Bowel Cancer called this a 'devastating decision'. If I had stayed in England it would have been devastating for me also. I am glad to report that the decision has subsequently been reversed.

Erbitux has many potential side effects, and these have to be managed in conjunction with those that may accrue from the chemotherapy. The most common one, from this particular monoclonal antibody, is an acne-like rash. I am told that the stronger the rash the stronger the success of the drug. I hold on to that thought as I come out in a severe rash all over and my face crumples in on itself, my eyelids puffing up.

Meanwhile, back in the real world, we have promised our daughter, Holly, that she can return to Belmont School, in London's district of Chiswick, to see all her friends again and celebrate the end of their final primary school year. This trip with Deirdre was part of the family negotiations prior to our return to Ireland and it cannot be reneged upon. Holly enjoys a happy reunion, although both she and Deirdre suffer the effects of a London heatwave, with temperatures rising to thirty-six degrees centigrade. Deirdre is also anxious about leaving me. She has a sixth sense.

The day after they depart for England, I have the unusual idea of making myself an egg mayonnaise salad for lunch. Don't ask me why. (For those readers of a squeamish disposition, or disinterested in the innermost workings of the human body, please feel free to turn the page or go for a walk at this point. For those of you who are fascinated by such things, you're in for a treat.)

After two mouthfuls of my carefully prepared meal, I literally dive towards the nearest toilet bowl. I am violently sick. My ribs crash involuntarily against the hard ceramic. Later in the evening the worst of the nausea has subsided and – I'll proceed as euphemistically as I am able to here – I need to sit on the loo for the usual reasons. I never knew that this was a possibility in life, but the next thing that happens is the sudden expulsion of large volumes of air out of the end of my penis. Like chronic flatulence but by the wrong route. At least there's no unpleasant odour; we may chalk that up as some kind of a blessing.

But, afterwards, I sit on the throne in shock. What new madness is this, I wonder? For once I do resort to Google, because I need to make sure that I'm not losing my mind.

Pneumaturia. That's apparently what it's called, when gas escapes via the urethra. It actually happens. I haven't gone insane. But that small reassurance doesn't make it any less bizarre a sensation.

By the time Deirdre and Holly arrive back with the Belmont School yearbooks, T-shirts, photos, London tans and other mementos, I have been chronically constipated for four days. I could also be useful in the pits of a Formula 1 motor race, inflating pneumatic Goodyear tyres with my own private parts compressor. To put it mildly, I'm not in the best of health and my wife is suitably concerned and upset.

We return to the A&E department of The Hospital, as the quickest means of entry. This time I introduce myself at the reception as one of their cancer patients: Number 0866248. 19-08-1965.

I'm whisked into my grey cell again in jig time. Another CT scan reveals that I have managed to conjure up a complication known as a fistula. Whether my passionate crunch with the toilet bowl caused it or not, nobody knows. But the tumour in the colon has now barged into my bladder and ruptured it. Hence, the separation of powers that should exist between the pipes for solid waste and the balloon for liquid excretions no longer stands. All is intermingled. The sanitation system is more liable to infection as a result.

I'm transferred back to my original ward, with a single room once more, but thankfully no view of the infernal golfers this time. I stay for several days awaiting a plan of action and living with the growing discomfort of my constipation and fistula. Junior doctors and registrars come and go, all advising me to get ready for surgery to fix this latest complication. They are not sure whether the operation to remove the colon cancer is also advisable now, in addition to fixing the fistula. Only Sean Martin, the expert colorectal surgeon from Tipperary, will be able to make that decision.

While I wait for news, I receive a visit from my oncologist, David Fennelly. He's comfortingly upbeat and as reassuring as he can be in the circumstances. 'It's obviously not ideal,' he says, 'to be pausing chemotherapy after only two sessions. And it's unlucky that this fistula has happened. But let's not worry, the after-effect of the chemotherapy drugs and the Erbitux will still be working away inside you, until you're able to resume.'

At least that's good to know, I suppose. Still, following the success of the liver operation, and the way Deirdre and I have planned a simple ticking of each medical box as it comes along, it's hard not to let my spirits dip a little.

Early on in this whole process, Anne White used a brilliant and appropriate description that I recall at this moment to boost my morale. 'You have to accept that this is not like fixing a car,' she had warned in the nicest possible way. 'It's so much more complicated than that and you need to be ready for all the variables and surprises that may arise. However, on each occasion that something unpredictable does occur, we will have other options for treatment and other ways to try to solve the problems.'

Fighting talk. I like it. So I embrace the idea that I am not as simple to fix as a car, even if I do now have a superhero's ability to inflate tyres with my cock.

It's a Friday afternoon, and I'm not looking forward to another weekend hospital slow-down. Sean Martin arrives. He is still wearing his blue scrubs and is fresh from the operating theatre, adrenaline pumping. I offer him a low-key acceptance that I know I need to have surgery to fix the fistula, and I ask whether he plans to do the colon cancer operation at the same time. As it turns out, I am completely on the wrong track. Full of energy and focus, Sean makes a decision that is diametrically opposed to all that I have been expecting from my conversations with his junior colleagues over the past few days.

'The most important thing,' he declares, 'is for you to continue with Dr Fennelly's chemotherapy. You're just going to have to put up with the confusions going on between bowels and bladder, and unless you come in here so ill that you really can't function, I don't want to see you again until you've finished the chemo. That is by far the most important course of action, in my opinion.'

This is a different side to Sean Martin, compared to the much quieter consultation of our first meeting. He is completely confident and pretty forceful. His attitude doesn't knock me backwards, even though dealing with the effects of the fistula for months does worry me. In fact, his perspective drives me forwards. It gives me another challenge. As for the consultant, he has one more important question for me. He wants to know what I have done with the metal stent that he inserted into my colon at the beginning of this whole process. Apparently, it's gone missing. I am given the impression that to pass it out by the obvious means would be like shitting a small roll of barbed wire, and I definitely would have noticed that. The latest CT scan has attested to its disappearance. I can't help with the mystery. I imagine a wave of admiration sweeping through the hospital staff. That guy, he passed a metal stent and he didn't even blink.

But I certainly do blink when, before he leaves, Sean prescribes a penetrative solution to the week-old constipation and instructs a nurse on the unenviable task of its execution. After a visit to my private facilities, and some bodily machinations that I respectfully decline to describe, I am purged and happily back at home in time for the *Six One News* on the TV.

***

Over the summer months, I manage to complete another three rounds of FOLFOX chemotherapy, with the accompanying

Erbitux immunotherapy. I have some more setbacks, just as most cancer patients do. On one occasion, I receive a phone call from a nurse to say that my latest blood tests have shown low levels of potassium. I reply glibly that I will drink some over-the-counter Dioralyte solution to increase them. Maybe eat some bananas too? Don't they have potassium in them? 'No,' I am told firmly, 'you need to come in to The Hospital for an intravenous drip.' That episode ends in a five-day stay. Apparently low potassium levels are potentially fatal. As my wife would say, every day's a school day.

During another week, I can't receive the infusion of chemotherapy because I am 'neutropenic'. This medical state happens when the white-blood-cell count drops and the immune system becomes very vulnerable. Again, a resulting sepsis can be lethal if the body suffers from high levels of infection. I don't feel worried or in danger on either occasion, because the doctors and nurses around me seem to be so in tune with the symptoms and signs. I always believe that they are ahead of the game in protecting me throughout the cycles of strong drugs. So I attempt to roll with the whole process and, much more importantly, I try to appreciate the attention lavished on me at home and the company of people I love. I see my children and family a lot, and Deirdre and I watch more television boxsets than we ever knew existed.

It isn't until the autumn, when I have been through five somewhat interrupted cycles of the FOLFOX and Erbitux, that I feel compelled to put my foot down. The fistula is having dire effects. I have reached the point of Sean Martin's exhortation where I feel I can't go on. I believe in my waters that, if I have another dose of the anti-cancer drugs, I will end up needing emergency surgery. I am worried that this would jeopardise all the progress that has been made. These are only a layman's conclusions, of course, but still I contact Anne White and ask her to express my concerns to the medical team in the strongest of terms. Maybe they are worried too, I never find out, but they agree to my request and discontinue the treatments.

Now I will need to have another CT scan, to see if any positive effect has been achieved in tackling my colon cancer and in keeping my liver and the rest of my body disease free. Sean Martin also needs to study the severity of the fistula, to plan for corrective surgery on my bladder. This is a particularly nerve-wracking time. I am poisoned and feeling very ill. Progress seems a distant horizon. I am at my most vulnerable, deep inside the underground caves.

MEETING

I was travelling overseas for work again.

It was the first time in three years. There were two trips to London within the space of a week. Something must have been happening. I spent several days in the enjoyable and intriguing company of Owen O'Neill, discussing ideas for his next draft of *The Safe*. Owen had left his native Ulster for England's capital several decades previously. This was the first time we had actually met in person since we decided to collaborate. Before that, communication had been contained in long emails, and unconfined in even longer and more energetic phone calls.

We soon settled down to the task at hand. Coffee was regularly ordered. We had recently received development funding to support us in our endeavours, so it was time to put a squeeze on the script. I poured out my thoughts on how to change and improve it, and Owen furiously scribbled down the notes. I had the easier job, because I was deconstructing the screenplay and pointing out queries and problems, without necessarily providing the answers. That would be the craftsman's job on the page: to solve all. At one point, during our three days of creative argy-bargy, I expressed my concern that this was a very bruising process. I had been through it myself as a screenwriter, after all, and knew the effect of the slings and arrows of other people's views upon the written work. Owen replied that he didn't see it that way but felt that this was more like the pieces of a jigsaw being thrown about with abandon. He embraced the chaos enthusiastically and we seemed to be seeing eye to eye, which is always an encouraging sign. We felt confident that the jigsaw pieces would ultimately fit together. However, the truth was that Owen had to be the one to fight the good fight, wrestling with the story and the scenes, in the privacy of his own headspace. It's always hard to know where that will lead, in the strange alchemy of putting pen to paper or fingers to keyboard. So I left him to it. Getting well out of his way.

My second trip to London that week was a brief one: a red-eye flight into London City Airport with my manager, Jane Russell. The last time I had been to that airport, the plane had screeched to a halt just before take-off and slewed across the runway. After a minute of silence, the pilot's shaky voice came over the tannoy: 'Sorry about that ladies and gentlemen, one of the engines wasn't quite doing what we wanted it to. So let's give it another try shall we?' And we did.

This flight was uneventful by comparison. Apart, that is, from Cillian Murphy's arrival on board at the last minute. He squeezed into the seat next to me. We spent a good deal of the journey reminiscing about George Martin and the evening we had spent in his apartment near Hyde Park, drinking his signature gin martinis and exchanging literal war stories in advance of the ill-fated production of *Wayfaring Strangers*. Meeting Cillian was a happy coincidence. The purpose of my day trip was to begin discussions about work on George Martin's book. Jane had organised a taxi into central London and we ejected Cillian at the Barbican Theatre, where he was going for rehearsals.

Ours was a flying visit to my favourite part of London – Soho. We were meeting Adam Sharp, George's manager, and also Norah Perkins, a London-based publishing agent. Norah decided that, because it was a Friday lunch meeting and we had an exciting project to discuss, she was going to launch proceedings by ordering a celebratory drink.

'I'll have a gin martini,' she said decisively to the waitress.

'Why did you order that?' I enquired, bemused by the coincidence of Norah ordering George's favourite drink.

'I have no idea,' Norah replied, laughing with slight embarrassment.

So now everyone at the meeting had to have one. For me, it would have been rude not to. New liver or no new liver. George Martin's orders.

Climbing back into my own Dublin bed that night, I switched on the *John Creedon Show*, to help me wind down. He was playing 'Strawberry Fields Forever', George's favourite

Beatles track. If this had been a sequence in a film, I would have been in trouble. By the rules of screenplay writing you're only allowed one coincidence. That was a bust. I'd had three in one day.

THURSDAY, 29 SEPTEMBER 2016

It's D-Day. Or, at least, CT Day. A reckoning.

I am in the twilight of the scanning room. I lie down on the machine and prepare to have dye pumped into a vein by the technologist, who gives me the warnings I have heard on previous occasions: 'You may have a hot flush, a metallic taste in your mouth and you will feel like you are going to pee. Except you won't.'

Thankfully, I don't experience any of those symptoms and this is actually a relatively gentle procedure. Not the same as the higher resolution MRI scan, which locks you into a claustrophobic tunnel and then bangs, shudders and shakes for half an hour, like an out-of-control bobsled with a police siren attached. The CT scan is all over in a few minutes. I'll have to wait about a week for the results and to find out whether my treatment is heading in the right direction. Usually the people operating the scans are poker-faced and give nothing away, which can be a little paranoia-inducing for the patient. They are under strict instructions to leave the imparting of results to the doctors. But on this occasion, the technologist can't resist a simple enquiry.

'Did you have something done to your liver?' she asks, sliding me back out of the scanner's arch.

I have to smile.

'I had half of it cut out four months ago,' I reply with an odd sense of pride. 'Why? How does it look now?'

'It looks great,' she enthuses. 'It's just a bit further over towards the middle than normal. But it all seems good.'

Hallelujah! The miracle of the human organ that is the liver, with its astonishing capacity to grow back to full size and drive the rest of the body's health along with it.

A week later, Deirdre and I go to meet David Fennelly. We wait nervously among others who are in similar boats, predicaments, states of trepidation and worried expectation. David greets us with a firm handshake and his trademark smile. He doesn't prolong the agony. He swings the computer screen around towards us so that we can see a cross-section of my body as he scrolls down through it on the black-and-white digital image: 'Listen, Stephen, your results are pretty good. As far as I can tell, the liver is now clear and the primary tumour in the colon has shrunk significantly. In fact, I can't really see it on the scan any more.'

Incredible news. Deirdre and I grab each other's hands and smile through a trace of wateriness in the eyes. The sense of relief is one of a kind and I am so grateful to this man sitting in front of me, whom I hardly know, but who has let us tick another box.

Of course, like everything on this unique pilgrimage, it's not without one more complication. 'The only thing that concerns me,' Dr Fennelly goes on, 'is that you still have some fluid collecting here, below the site of the liver operation. We don't like to see that. It's not good. That fluid could contain cancerous cells. And Sean Martin isn't going to agree to operate on the primary tumour until he's sure that's not the case. So we're going to have to extract a sample of that liquid. To see what's going on.'

Add another box to be ticked.

***

Even though there's still a long way to travel, I am becoming very hopeful and optimistic now. But I've grown an extra antenna. At every medical procedure I undergo, I am now in a state of heightened awareness, watching all the preparations and machinations like a hawk. It's a response that surprises me. It feels a bit like the metamorphosis that I undergo when I am directing a film. I become obsessive, agitated, energetic and manically determined. I'm not like that in any other walk of my life. I tend to be a bit passive, facilitating of others' demands: a little too much so for my own good, I can hear my darling wife say. But I'm changing.

The difference in this arena, of course, is that I have no expertise. I have to surrender to the specialists. I'm more than willing to do that, considering how carefully they have treated me until now. Nevertheless, I'm focusing on them intensely. I'm scrutinising every move. So, a few days later, when it comes to having this possibly cancerous fluid drawn from deep in my innards, I'm on tenterhooks. I know that the site where the extremely long needle has to be inserted is very close to my fistula. That little bollocks has been giving me much less trouble since I stopped having the chemotherapy. I wouldn't even be able to blow up a small balloon now, let alone a car's tyre. So I am keen to keep it that way.

A nurse sets me up on a trolley for the procedure, known as an aspiration. It's not one that I really aspire to, but hey-ho it has to be done. In comes a young doctor with a large handbag on a gold-coloured chain slung over her shoulder. She doesn't remove the bag as she puts gel on my pelvic area and starts to search around with the ultrasound machine. My antenna thinks that this is simply odd, and I quickly raise my concerns. 'You do know that I have a fistula very near there?' I say to her, pointing to the image on the ultrasound. 'I'm very anxious that nothing is done to worsen that.'

She immediately leaves to get the next doctor in the chain of command. The new entrant is more senior and definitely more confident. This doctor spends a long time ultrasounding. She says that the volume of fluid available to draw out is very small and that, in the overall scheme of things, this could be a good sign because my body is reabsorbing it. But I can tell that it will make her task of withdrawing fluid with the long aspiration needle much more difficult.

I ask her very directly if she can reach the fluid without exacerbating the damage already done by the fistula. It's the new, pushy me. Maybe I'm learning some new survival skills in life. Clearly doctor number two isn't overly confident and takes time to consider her answer. That's fine by me. Finally, she says that I may need to have surgery in order to access the sample.

Obviously, I want to avoid that.

'Is there anyone else in the house?' I enquire, as politely as I can.

I am left alone with the nurse once more. Then the senior registrar charges in. No messing. She's probably heard that I've been a bit bolshie. We're clearly in business, as the registrar sweeps her hand quickly through the gel with the head of the ultrasound. She readies the aspiration needle as I desperately try to catch up with events.

'Is there enough liquid there for you to get a sample?'

'Yes. Just about.'

'Can you please give me some anaesthetic, before you take the plunge?'

'Yes. Just a small local one. Right here.'

She injects the painkiller, followed immediately by the long straight aspiration needle deep into my insides. The anaesthetic has no time to take effect. My whole body arches with a reflex action at the excruciating pain. My arm swings up involuntarily and punches the doctor in the midriff.

'Sorry,' I say with incongruous good manners. The old me. Back again.

The registrar parries the blow and pulls the needle out, swiftly and victoriously, like the sword in *Excalibur* (dir. John Boorman, 1981).

'Did you get what you needed?' I gasp.

'Yes. I did.'

And she's gone, in a cloud of mystical, medical mist.

***

Two days later I'm at home, lying in bed early in the morning. I can hear Holly and Daniel getting ready for school in the normal noisy, chaotic fashion. My mobile phone rings. That is an unusual occurrence in itself, because I have cut off most telephone conversations over the past few months: as a matter of choice, of necessity, of sanity, isolating me from unpredictable communication and unidentified callers who may upset my equilibrium.

On this occasion I do answer.

'Hello, Stephen?'

'Yes.'

'It's David Fennelly here.'

My heart jumps.

I sit to attention because there's a figure of authority on the line. Old me.

'Ah, David. Good morning.'

'Those tests have come back from the lab. On the fluid that was extracted, during the aspiration procedure.'

'Oh. Right. And?'

'They were negative. All clear. No trace of any cancer cells there.'

My heart lifts.

'That's fantastic news, David.'

'Yes. It's very good. Well done.'

'Well done yourself. Thanks so much for the call.'

'No problem. You can get on with the next stage of your treatment now. The colon surgery with Sean Martin. I'll see you soon.'

I leap out of bed and shout the latest information downstairs to Deirdre.

'Of course the tests were clear,' my wife says in typical fashion. 'I knew they would be. Would you like a cup of tea?'

A cup of tea.

Now that I really do aspire to.

EXILING

In 2018, I finally met Emperor Napoleon again. I knew he was coming; I had been waiting for him. I had met him once before.

The last of the many film festivals that I attended with *Noble* was in the intriguing city of Ajaccio, in Corsica. I flew into Paris and made my connection onwards to the large French island in the Mediterranean. My trip, in December 2015, was only a month after the dreadful, murderous attacks on the Stade de France and Bataclan Theatre. The armed police presence was heightened at Charles de Gaulle Airport. There was a brief panic next to me, while I waited for my second flight. Some unthinking fool had decided that he would navigate the zig-zag of the security queue by abandoning his heavy bag at each turn, to retrieve it when he came past that point again. People scattered when the unattended bag was suddenly noticed. The airport police went berserk with the witless passenger, once the method in his madness had been discovered. Then everyone in the fractured queue was able to breathe a sigh of relief again.

I had always wanted to go to Corsica, but I didn't know why. When our French distributor, Hugues Peysson, heard about this yearning, he kindly arranged for the entry of *Christina Noble*, as the film is called in France, to the Corsican festival. I knew nothing about the island, beyond the schoolboy knowledge that it was Emperor Napoleon Bonaparte's birthplace.

I had a window seat on the plane and looked below as we banked over its craggy, jagged rocks and foaming sea, glowing crimson in the winter sunset. It was easy to imagine the sailors and pirates who had undoubtedly foundered there over centuries gone by. My quaint hotel room faced onto ancient grassy battlements, now the preserve of two donkeys, who conducted a braying competition between themselves for the duration of my stay. The film festival itself was small but well attended, and the passionate organisers looked after the film-makers hospitably, as they so often do. They were happy to provide me with a potted history of the island, and seemed most proud of the fact that it had regularly played host to revolutionaries from all over the world, at a secret annual *rendezvous* deep in the mountainous interior. They delighted in telling me that one notorious Irish Republican, who had attended the get-together of political dissidents in the 1970s, had become so paralytically drunk that he had been unable to deliver his keynote address. As for me, the festival hosts brought me to a traditional Corsican feast of such rich and voluminous portions that I was also unable to stay the course. Needless to say, in retrospect, I now know why I was struggling. Within four months I would be hospitalised. My innards were already in a bad way.

I visited Napoleon's childhood home, discreetly preserved as a museum. Then I sought out Ajaccio's stone monument to him. It stands as a sleek form, rising impressively with the emperor himself cast atop it in bronze glory, his bicorn hat silhouetted unmistakably against the pale blue of the Corsican sky. The whole sojourn had a strong impact on me, clearly indulging as I was in the romanticism of the place.

Prior to one of my longer stays in The Hospital during my illness, I raided the local library for reading material to sustain me during my incarceration. One of the books was a novella, part of an expanding fictional genre that speculated on gaps in Napoleonic history. This revisionist new wave propagated interesting conspiracy theories and fantasies, particularly about the end of the emperor's days. There was no shortage of books and films on the subject. But I discovered one in particular that caught my interest, as I continued my research at home, nestling into the next bout of enforced recuperation.

Napoleon in Exile; or, A Voice from St Helena was published as two lengthy volumes in 1822, written by Napoleon's personal doctor, Barry O'Meara. He was one of two Irishmen who featured in Napoleon's final and most uncomfortable years, banished on the island of St Helena, in the middle of the South Atlantic Ocean. It was a place 'shat by the devil between two worlds', according to one of Napoleon's long-suffering entourage. The other Hibernian character in this remarkable moment in history was the governor of the isolated island, Sir Hudson Lowe. He was born in Galway. Although, as the talented man I am about to introduce describes it so succinctly: 'Hudson Lowe wasn't bothered by his Irishness and tried to hide it at every turn.'

***

Jonathan White, actor and writer, came to my rescue once. In 2005, the comedy-horror film I had directed, *Boy Eats Girl*, was refused a certificate by the Office of the Irish Censor, effectively banning it from any form of distribution. Out of the blue, and certainly through no prompting from me, Jonathan wrote an elegant but excoriating letter against the decision, which was prominently published in *The Irish Times*. The late Gerry Ryan also supported the cause on his radio show, and the film was eventually given a censorship certificate on appeal, which allowed its release into the cinemas. Although I hardly knew him, Jonathan White was then firmly on my radar as a brave and principled stalwart friend to those in need.

Much later, I was delighted when he accepted a small but crucial role in *Noble*, and he flew to Liverpool where we were shooting his court-room scene. Somehow, I have always been aware of a deep well of intelligence and ability in Jonathan.

This was long before his most recent success touring Ireland and Britain with a play he has co-written, called *To Hell in a Handbag*. It was also prior to the considerable behind-the-scenes assistance he has provided for his wife, Anne Clarke, who is currently Ireland's most successful and dynamic theatre producer.

In mid-2018, Jonathan and I sat down in one of the regular meeting places I like to call an office, the excellent Leonardo's Coffee Shop. I told him about Barry O'Meara's book, expressing my fascination with the story of Napoleon Bonaparte and the two Irishmen. Jonathan's eyes lit up and the geek historian, a part of him that I did not yet know about, came bursting into life.

After that, he did months of research in between his other projects. This included reading both volumes of the Irish physician's nineteenth-century account of his close relationship with the former emperor. Then Jonathan started to tell me about the beginnings of his tantalising writing for a prospective film. We walked the stone pier, part of an important ritual in my life, and he brought me into the world of his story. It was full of jaded finery, dilapidated houses, a doomed coterie of the once-powerful, sexual intrigue and reckless violence, plans for escape and returns to past triumphs. With wine and comic asides. Lots of wine and comic asides, to both dull and lift the senses during this godforsaken end to an emperor who once ruled the world.

Jonathan and I hardly noticed the wind and freezing rain, against which neither of us was well attired. It was as if we were transported there, to grim and monstrous St Helena, two centuries prior. I had finally met Napoleon again. And I knew that it wouldn't be the last time. He was a much-appreciated late entry into the race.

MONDAY, 17 OCTOBER 2016

I have now been having treatment for exactly six months.

I keep an appointment in a department of The Hospital that is completely new to me. There I meet a brilliantly energetic specialist nurse, Brid O'Neill.

'So, there's no lovely way to put this, Stephen,' she says with a smile. 'We need to make you a new bum-hole.'

Welcome to the world of the stoma. In order to by-pass the large colon, giving it time to heal after the next operation that will cut out my primary tumour, the medics introduce me to a whole new way to poo. Hopefully it won't be permanent and normal rectal service will resume at some indeterminate point in the future. But for now I have to get used to a different level of intimacy with my own body.

At my very first chemotherapy session the oncology nurse said to me:

'People laugh at us when we have such an obsessive and constant interest in their bowels. But that's because, medically speaking, we can tell so much from the guts.'

The further this journey progresses, the more I realise this claim to be true, and the more I understand the importance and effect of everything we ingest and digest. Somewhere along the way I think that we in the 'West' may have lost the awareness of this, because our ancestors certainly knew it. In many other cultures they know it still. As a child, I was innately embarrassed by all things gut and tract related. The latest version of me has no chance of maintaining even a tiny modicum of such innocent reticence, however, because I am about to get a new bum-hole. I will have to learn to love it and look after it. It's a hole new world.

Brid explains what is involved in this part of the surgery, known as an ileostomy. It's very simple and a little astonishing. It also makes you wonder what kind of crazy surgeon came up with the idea in the first place. As I know that there is general enthusiasm among the populace to hear all about it, let me describe it in some detail. An incision is made in the abdomen wall and a 'loop' of the small intestine is pulled out through the new orifice. This is cut open and stitched into position like a huge, permanently moist, nipple (it's now called a stoma), so that bodily waste can be collected in a specially designed disposable bag, stuck over it like a limpet on a rock. I am very excited by the prospect of having this done, as I'm sure everyone can tell. But it's another box to be ticked, and for that I can only be thankful.

Brid does the difficult, potentially embarrassing, job of explaining all this with great expertise, as well as with doses of her native Carlow black humour. Laughing is probably the only way to go and that's exactly what we do. Then we discuss more important things, like how much Brid fancies Harvey Specter in the television series *Suits*, which we are both consuming voraciously on Netflix. Meghan Markle, who plays Rachel Zane in the legal drama, hasn't even started dating Prince Harry yet. We are so ahead of the times, my stoma nurse and me.

I am on a brief hiatus before the colorectal surgeon, Sean Martin, undertakes the next major operation in three weeks' time. These days are a glimpse of the future I am trying to achieve. I have escaped from the worst side effects of the chemotherapy and immunotherapy. I am starting to feel a little sunshine inside, a fleeting sense of what it is like to feel well, that glorious nirvana that we all take for granted when it is ours. Soon I will have to surrender it again. In the meantime, I'm doing what any sensible person would do: I'm going to Disneyland.

For fear of over-excited, sleepless nights, we don't tell our children until half an hour before the taxi comes to take us all to the airport. Daniel, who was eight last month, has been promised this trip for a long time. Holly, now eleven, is approaching the advanced age when she might soon baulk at such frivolity. I'm fifty-one and clinging on. It's now or never.

We booked the plane tickets ages ago, not having a clue whether or not I would be able to travel. Once it becomes apparent that I am going to have this small window between the chemo and the scalpel, we forge ahead and book the expensive bits: a couple of nights in the hotel with Donald Duck carpets and Goofy staring down from the bedroom wallpaper, as well as entry into Paris's finest literary salon, Disneyland itself. It proves no more surreal an experience than the rest of our life at the moment. A great time is had by all. Well, what did you expect when I'm still on the opiates?

***

If I feel some strength being restored to my body, I also feel my mind waking up. Not only am I anxious to get back to writing and directing, but I am also aware that my mental well-being and spiritual exploration mustn't be forgotten. Indeed they won't allow themselves to be neglected. They are banging the door down, shouting demands and catcalling: that if I don't discover some meaning behind this bodily mayhem then it will all come to naught. Perhaps, my mind warns, I won't survive if I don't find some answers and some peace.

I start to read and search. Everyone around me helps with suggestions and conversations about whatever it is that drives them on, inspires them, or makes them feel calm. One of the first things I discover is that the dietary part of this really isn't just mumbo-jumbo. Amazon's share price starts to rise with the number of books I order. One of the first to arrive is *Anti-*

cancer: A New Way of Life, written by a French doctor called David Servan-Schreiber. Being of an irritatingly sceptical nature, I like material on this subject to have been written by a doctor, or at least a research scientist. Servan-Schreiber, who is both, also has an interesting personal story. As a high-flying young researcher in Pittsburgh, he and two other medics were given night-time access to the hospital's precious and newly invented MRI scanner, in order to pursue their investigations into brain function. One evening a post-graduate student, who they were using as a guinea pig, failed to show up. Dr Servan-Schreiber volunteered to take his place and boarded the scanner. There was silence from his colleagues, however, as he started to undergo the experiments. They had seen a large tumour in his brain. He was thirty years old. He underwent successful surgery but did nothing afterwards to change his lifestyle or mental attitude. The cancer returned. This time, after aggressive chemotherapy and a period of remission, Servan-Schreiber was determined to keep it away. He started collating all the available research on dietary impact for most forms of cancer and published it in his book. He also started eating and drinking what he preached. David lived for another fifteen years and put much of that time down to the changes he made and the mental improvements that were a natural part of such a rigorous routine.

Servan-Schreiber refers to another book that he likes. I note that it is being published in an updated version in a couple of months' time. I pre-order it, feeling very smug that I will now have the very latest dietary ammunition. This one is called *Foods to Fight Cancer* and it is written by the sceptic-proof double whammy of Professor Richard Béliveau and Dr Denis Gingras. It's a colourful encyclopedia of foodstuffs, outlining their supposed negative or positive effect on different cancers, with statistical charts, graphs and figures to reassure or warn. Some of the propositions are startling in their simplicity. Turmeric, a spice mainly used to make curry and with proven anti-inflammatory properties, is apparently partially responsible for Indian men having ninety per cent less likelihood of developing colon cancer than men eating a 'Western diet'. When Indians move to the latter regime, the book says, their risk of getting cancer increases dramatically. Green tea, especially the Japanese varieties, is another very accessible product for which great claims are made. And the list goes on: tomatoes cooked in olive oil; berries of as many colours as possible; garlic and onions; broccoli, cabbage and Brussels sprouts; soya; oily fish; red wine and dark chocolate. Educating myself about diet is also good for my mental health. I am trying to live for a future that I had once naively presumed was already ahead of me. Now I have to make changes to achieve that future. I'll take advice from all quarters and see what I feel about it in my gut.

My father's lifelong friend Eamon McEnery once phoned me out of the blue and said: 'Anyone who lives in the countryside, and witnesses what happens during the springtime, knows that there is a higher power.' I have always remembered that sentence and it seems like a good place for my present ruminations to start. Paki Smith mentions a book called *Man's Search for Meaning* by the famed Austrian psychotherapist Viktor Frankl. If the title is very apt, the book is even more extraordinary. In it, Frankl describes his experience of living in Nazi concentration camps for three years, mostly in Auschwitz. He discusses the reasons why some people in his 'working party' survived, while others did not. He candidly admits that he was prepared to use every available means to save himself, while others couldn't or wouldn't: 'We who have come back, by the aid of lucky chances or miracles – whatever one may choose to call them – we know: the best of us did not return.'[1]

I visited Auschwitz in 1995 when I attended a film festival in nearby Krakow. Now the chilling reality of what happened in that concentration camp is brought home to me again, as is the enduring and often unexpected strength of the human spirit. Quoting Nietzsche, Frankl explains a crucial aspect of that phenomenon, illustrated through his own experience in the camps: 'He who has a *why* to live for can bear with almost any *how*.'[2]

---

1 Frankl, Victor E., *Man's Search for Meaning* (Rider, Great Britain, 2008), p. 19.
2 *Ibid.*

When I initially received my cancer diagnosis I knew that it was very serious, but, for the same reason that I stayed away from Internet research, I decided not to ask for the official medical labelling. I didn't want to know that it was rightly described as stage IV colon cancer, metastasised to a large secondary liver tumour. Nor did I want to be informed that my blood tumour markers, which in a healthy patient should be in a range between 0.7 and 5, were topping out at 1,300. So I didn't ask.

I distinctly recall my gastroenterologist, Juliette Sheridan, saying to me at the time: 'You have a lot to live for.' It was a simple but inspiring thing to hear. In particular, I have a lot of people to live for: my children, my wife and her extended family; my sister and her family; my parents, who I remember clutching each other as Fiona's coffin was lowered, which is not an experience I want them to repeat with another of their offspring; and my own circle of valued friends and other relations.

Over the coming weeks, I become extremely determined and positive about the future. Which is just as well, because Dr Servan-Schreiber tells me in his book that, by entering this mental state, I am increasing the number of natural killer (NK) cells in my blood, and that they are vital for the battle ahead.

There is another important moment that stays with me from Victor Frankl's story. Under armed guard at Auschwitz in mid-winter, he is digging a trench with a pickaxe and writes that he's also 'struggling to find a *reason* for these sufferings'. He hears a loud voice in his head telling him that, YES, there is an answer to his question about the existence of an ultimate purpose. As he toils all day in the freezing cold, he spiritually communes with his beloved wife, not knowing whether she is alive or dead in some other Nazi hellhole. He becomes so mentally entwined with her that he believes he feels her presence, almost sensing the touch of her hand. 'Then, at that very moment,' Frankl writes, 'a bird flew down silently and perched just in front of me, on the heap of soil which I had dug up from the ditch, and looked steadily at me.'[3] Frankl refers to such instances as 'a hint from Heaven'.[4]

Another book I read is *Catching the Big Fish: Meditation, Consciousness, and Creativity*, by the film-maker David Lynch. I have been fascinated by him ever since I watched his first feature film, *Eraserhead*, in Lake Placid, New York, just after the end of my student theatre tour, in 1988. His book is beautifully simple and poetic, describing moments of great impact on his life and espousing the benefits of Transcendental Meditation, which he has practised twice a day for most of his adulthood. He says of the technique: 'it's bliss – physical, emotional, mental and spiritual happiness that starts

---

3   *Ibid.*, p. 52.
4   *Ibid.*, p. 13.

growing from within.'[5] I'm going to have some of that. It would be foolish not to. So I'm booking myself in for a course.

At one point in Lynch's writing, he describes a period when he was wrestling unsuccessfully with the ideas he wanted to portray in *Eraserhead*. He took out his Bible for inspiration and suddenly found a single sentence that completed his vision. 'I don't think I'll ever say what that sentence was,' is his way of frustrating us all.[6] When Fiona was given her diagnosis of terminal secondary cancer, I too had opened a Bible at a random page to find wisdom and reassurance. It wasn't there. I felt idiotic and childish.

***

I have always struggled with religious labels. When I was much younger, truly childish, it didn't make sense to me that, for centuries, people's supposed religion was, and in some places still is, largely dictated by the accident of their birth or upbringing. I couldn't comprehend how a genuine spiritual belief system could be dictated by geography or genealogy.

I was brought up in a Protestant family in the Republic of Ireland, where ninety-seven per cent of people declared as Roman Catholic. To the logic of my young mind, that was

---

5   Lynch, David, *Catching the Big Fish: Meditation, Consciousness, and Creativity* (Penguin Random House, USA, 2016), p. 51.

6   *Ibid.*, p. 33.

just a fact of historical evolution, not a meaningful spiritual victory for one denomination of Christianity over another in advance of the Second Coming.

I also had to reconcile myself with the fact that Protestantism in the Republic of Ireland has often been treated as being inseparable from the political stigma of British colonialism, and often carried with it the derogatory label of 'West Brit'. As a child, I noticed that this bias was regularly disguised by supposedly affectionate comic asides. But, in truth, there was no use of the term that was not pejorative. I found that difficult to swallow. At times, like all kids wanting to fit in, I longed to be part of the majority. As I perceived it, to be more Irish than I was allowed to be. This despite the fact that, ironically, the Christian denomination that I was baptised into is called the Church of Ireland.

I have a strong memory of moving into a new house in Dublin at the age of fourteen, and of a local Roman Catholic priest visiting to welcome us, only to be told good-humouredly by my father that 'we are of the other persuasion'.

The truth is that I am not of any persuasion, which is not the same thing as saying that I am an atheist. So perhaps that is the answer: that this life should be a constant spiritual journey, made more urgent by serious illness and enforced contemplation about the end of one's time on earth.

I think that Turkish writer Elif Shafak puts it well in her episode of *Desert Island Discs*. She says that she doesn't feel close to organised religions because they all have a dualistic assumption, one against the other, that '*us* is closer to the truth than *them*'. However, Shafak also says that she is very interested in the possibility of God: 'What I like is individual spiritual journeys. And those journeys are plural. Everybody's journey will be different, like their fingerprints. So you might be interested in Islamic mysticism; you might end up closer to Jewish mysticism. You might start in one bay and swim to other shores. Anything is possible because those paths are based on that individual's features and needs.'[7]

Thankfully, from my point of view, there are some inte-resting and nourishing stories along the way. My sister-in-law, Liz O'Kane, introduces me to the fascinating and unusual life of John Sullivan. I watch a moving documentary about him and his work, right up to the time of his death in 1933. He was born into a middle-class Protestant family in Dublin, studied law at Trinity College and then went off on a European tour, as people of such social standing did in those days. He almost died of smallpox in London while qualifying as a barrister. Then he returned to Ireland and, in a very unusual conversion for the time, became a Roman Catholic Jesuit priest. He lived an austere life as a teacher at Clongowes Wood College and spent his spare time visiting the poor and the sick, just as he had apparently done while he was a lawyer. Fr John Sullivan

7   BBC Radio 4, *Desert Island Discs*, 28 May 2017.

is credited with several cases of outright healing. Evidence of these alleged miracles is needed for him to be canonised into sainthood under the rules of the Roman Catholic Church. (After an investigative process dating back to 1944, he was beatified in May 2017 and became officially known as Blessed John Sullivan.) Liz has given me a relic that is a fragment of John's clothing and believes that, after all her entreaties on my behalf, he will have a hand in healing me. How can you not be grateful for that, and humbled by it?

I am gratified to hear of friends and family praying and lighting candles for me, all over the world. My brother-in-law, Rory O'Reilly, lends me a treasured silver angel pendant in a presentation box and the password for his Sky Sports subscription. Giles Martin couriers me the latest Sonos speaker, which he has designed to sit under the television. It makes the Sky Sports come alive. A great friend from our Chiswick days, Professor Becky Earley, sends me an online surprise of a Deepak Chopra recording with words set to music: *The Secret of Healing – Meditations for Transformation and Higher Consciousness*. For many months I listen to it intermittently, and wrestle to understand its wisdoms. It gives me great pleasure and comfort. I am also blessed with three bottles of Holy Water from Lourdes, Russia and some other indeterminate but equally important place.

Another sister-in-law, Grainne O'Kane, passionately researches the power of essential oils that are extracted from plants and fruits, presented in a very concentrated, pure form. She tells me that there are trials being conducted at the Mayo Clinic in America and that conventional medicine is, if reluctantly, showing some interest in claims that certain oils are clinically effective against a range of diseases. Grainne is very knowledgeable on the subject and we go through a period of months during which, because she is temporarily staying in our house, she massages the strong oils into my feet, hands and temples. It's unbelievably relaxing and therapeutic. Grainne says that frankincense, in particular, has strong anti-cancer properties and she gives me a lovely little bottle of the precious stuff.

Suzie drives me to and from The Hospital on my many, many visits and we have enjoyable, always therapeutic, discussions about our life and times. Her husband, Pete, assumes the very important task of putting up our Christmas tree when I am clearly unable to fulfil that traditional role. Pamela, a professional genealogist and historian, brings me fascinating snippets of information about our ancestors and their wild and sometimes wonderful lives. I walk on the stone pier, stretching far into Dublin Bay, and every time I do I remember Brendan's grandfather, Joseph. He worked as a postal sorter on the RMS *Leinster,* a ship that set sail from this very harbour in 1918. It was hit by a German submarine's torpedoes, twelve miles out, near the Kish Lighthouse. Joseph was one of around 565 passengers and crew who were killed in that dreadful ordeal. There is a photograph of him in the local post office, and I bring his great-great-grandchildren, Holly and Daniel, in to see it.

I am also grateful that, unlike Viktor Frankl, I don't have to summon my wife in my imagination. Deirdre is here beside me every moment of this journey. Not only does she keep me focused and in a positive frame of mind (a tearful diversion from that path might occasionally be permitted but only for a maximum of five minutes), she also tells me continually that she *knows* that I will be cured. If I believe in one thing, it's that I can't argue with her. And, if you knew my wife and the strength of her soul, neither would you.

In any case, before I get completely carried away, it's time to surrender this distracted, spring-like feeling, rising up in me after all that contemplation.

I have to walk back through the doors of The Hospital.

Another operating theatre is waiting for me.

Another six hours under the knife.

Another lifesaver.

LISTENING

On some days, it was just all about me. Everything else took a back seat.

I often enjoyed taking Daniel and Holly to their respective schools early in the mornings, before a desk-bound stretch of screen or book writing. After dropping the boy off first, I drove into lush and leafy Wicklow for the second set-down. I then returned from the girl's school on a tiny, twisty back road. It was a regular thoroughfare that I used in my twenties, and was now not known by the drivers of cars streaming along the adjacent motorway. The journey with the children was a simple pleasure – even if I had to put up with a selection of banal pop songs in constant rotation on the radio until I was alone again.

Alone again, and finally in control of the airwaves, I listened to the *Morning Ireland* news programme. I happened to hear an interview with my oncologist, Dr David Fennelly. He was bravely picking up the pieces after the exposure of drastic flaws in some cervical cancer screening cases. He was responding to a damning investigative report on past laboratory shortcomings, and the unacceptable behaviour of a few clinicians. It had fallen to David to take the flak for the failures and omissions of others. Answering the journalist's questions he was as clear, informative and compassionate as I have always found him to be. But it can't have been easy for him. He was representing his profession in a febrile atmosphere. Women's lives had been unnecessarily and tragically lost, high-profile compensation cases settled, the general public generally appalled. There was an accusation that a culture of arrogance had been fostered in previous generations of medics, who did not feel that patients deserved proper communication or even access to their personal case files. As a result, there was now a backlash against the medical fraternity as a whole.

It has to be said that, in the vast majority of cases, doctors deserve the respect they have been afforded since topping their exams at school, garnering impossible numbers of points to enter universities, undergoing at least seven to ten years of training, then taking sabbaticals and placements around the world to gain experience and bring it all back home. For a child to become a doctor was and is every parent's pride. I had experienced that feeling as an onlooker, during the academic and Hippocratic journey of my own sister, Fiona.

It's a tough profession and the responsibilities are onerous. Gallows humour is often necessary for medic, patient and public alike, as relief from the constant pressure. By way of illustration, here's my favourite medical gag: the well-known

British performer, Sanjeev Bhaskar, described the response when he told his parents that he was going to become an actor. His father replied wryly:

'It's pronounced *doctor*.'

My serious face returned. Visiting The Hospital, as I still regularly did for scans, blood tests and consultations, I could sense the change in the atmosphere; it seemed a place under siege. Anecdotally, members of the medical staff were naturally more defensive, while patients were more demanding and Google-happy in their enquiries.

Of course, there were public policy issues that needed to be urgently dealt with, and public relations improvements that were long overdue. Female cancer patients, cruelly impacted by the cervical smear scandal, emerged courageously as leaders of progress. The discourse was opened up to the media, as well as water coolers, coffee shops and dinner tables. It was an important and cleansing airing of views, and a difficult, daring challenge to the status quo that forced politicians to take note and respond with action.

But, from a very personal point of view, I found that it didn't make for easy listening:

It made me constantly aware of my own cancer.

It made me anxious about the morale of my own medical team.

It made me paranoid about if or when my cancer would return.

It made me drift occasionally into the darkness.

It made me wonder when I was going to die, on what day and what date.

It made me think that I had been blessed in some unfathomable way.

It made me realise that I used the possessive form *my* oncologist.

'I'll try to behave myself,' I said to Fennelly, with a grin, after a clear scan.

'Don't,' he said wisely. 'Go and enjoy yourself.'

On a later occasion he encouraged me to just keep going and, at another moment of helpful motivation, he said that he expected to be managing me for a long time. I decided that I should ask him when he was going to retire. I reasoned that if I could make it to his retirement party, many years in the future (whether invited or – more probably – not), then I would have been anxious and paranoid for no reason.

On some days, it was just all about me.

Everything else took a back seat.

FRIDAY, 11 NOVEMBER 2016

On the day of my second major surgery, I am instructed to be at The Hospital early in the morning. I am hoping that this will mean I am first up on the surgical list. Deirdre and I drive over there, while Suzie brings Holly and Daniel to school for us. It's a difficult parting as I say farewell to my children. My beautiful Holly, almost a teenager now and certainly beginning to act like one, manages a nonchalant goodbye and good luck. Eight-year-old Daniel gives me a big embrace, looks me straight in the eye and tells me that he loves me. He seems, instinctively, to know more than he has been told. He later informs me that, every day while I was in hospital, he sat at the bottom of the stairs and waited for me to come home. Today, it's hard to keep my emotions in check, but I don't want him to see any tears, or to reveal any fears.

We arrive at The Hospital and it looks like we may be in luck, first in the queue. Brid, my stoma nurse, is in typically cheerful mood and leads me away to a side room. She takes out a large felt-tip pen and draws a thick black cross onto the skin at the right side of my tummy, so that the surgeon will know exactly where the stoma is to be positioned, above the line of my trouser belt. I am literally a marked man.

Deirdre and I lie on the bed in a waiting room. We resume our habit of doing the *Irish Times* crossword together. 'You can relax for a while,' says a ward nurse, as she pokes her head around the door, a little embarrassed that we are already in that compromised position of relaxation. 'You'll be last into surgery today, I'm afraid. They've just realised from your notes that you have the VRE infection. They'll need to do all the listed surgery before you, so as not to risk infecting the other patients.'

The symptom-less superbug has come back to haunt me. 'Once VRE, always VRE!' the nurse hollers, as she leaves us to a much longer wait. Someone else arrives with the surgical consent form for me to sign. Yes, I do know about the risks associated with the general anaesthetic and operation. Yes, I am aware that death is a possible consequence under certain circumstances. But I'm really hoping to stick around for a while longer.

All things considered, I'm surprisingly calm. I think that these situations are much worse for your family members than they are for you. General anaesthetics are a complete knock-out. You don't have dreams like you do in normal sleep. So, one minute you're awake and then the next minute you're waking up again. There's nothing in between. Certainly not the hours and hours of anxious waiting time that Deirdre and my family are about to go through. Because there's a lot of work to be done: removing the section of the large colon that is cancerous, along with a generous margin of 'good' tissue, to be safe; reconnecting the two healthy ends of that particular digestive tube; cutting out a portion of the bladder, where the tumour has damaged it and caused the fistula; re-sealing it to watertight standards (my colorectal surgeon, Sean Martin, tells me that he has asked a consultant urologist to assist him on this section of the procedure, as an extra insurance policy); creating the stoma, as previously described, providing me with my own little model of the volcano at Vesuvius that will erupt with its own uniquely unpleasant lava flow; and finally, the extraction of between twenty and thirty lymph nodes from all around the surgical site, so that they can be tested in the pathology laboratory to discover whether cancer has infected my lymph system.

I kiss my worried wife and try to smile reassuringly as my hospital trolley is wheeled away, through code-protected security doors. Up in the elevator I go, to the surgical floor, and I am parked briefly in the reception area. A nurse I know (that's becoming a long list by now) shimmies by and tells me the latest news: Adrian, my Welsh intensive care angel after the liver resection, has just celebrated the arrival of his first baby. He'll be fine, I tell her; he's used to being up all night. I ask the nurse to send my congratulations. Then the trolley is back into gear, motoring into the operating theatre.

No needle in the spine this time, just a simple cannula inserted into the arm, and an oxygen mask over mouth and nose. Sean Martin arrives to speak to me before I conk out. He circles the surgical table, surveying the scene, and we wish each other a simple 'Good luck!'

The anaesthetist moves in for the kill.

Nothingness.

.

.

.

.

***

I wake up in a small single room.

I have all the usual tubes, valves, wires and drains, with the addition of a disposable stoma bag. Refills of this will be my constant companion for the next year, and could double for a Hoover bag on the Telios S3420 model.

During the following days, as I lie in my hospital bed, I have a catheter permanently inserted into my penis. It reaches up inside, as far as my bladder, and urine is diverted to a see-through plastic box with markings on it, like a measuring jug. The Hoover bag collects anything more solid. I also have a large plastic tube that is channelling all manner of liquids from the very core of my being into a translucent heavy-duty pouch. This drains the internal site of the operation and provides the surgeon with forensic clues as to the success or otherwise of his handiwork. Bags of antibiotics and saline hang overhead, completing the fluid situation, with a patient-controlled morphine pump in play once more as well.

Unknown to me, Deirdre has already had a detailed conversation with Sean Martin, as the next of kin is entitled to do. He has informed her that he needed to cut away much more of my bladder than had been foreseen, in order to provide safe margins from the cancer tissue that had barged in on top of it. Deirdre asked him what this extra extraction might mean in practical terms. Sean told her that he wasn't sure yet, but that, in the worst-case scenario, it could lead to lifelong incontinence, or even the necessity for a permanent external drainage bag. My wife had to keep that grim prospect to herself as I came round from the operation and began the long healing process.

You'd think that my bed-ridden visceral state, awash with the essences and excretions of life, would be as far away as I could get from my obsession with films, but you'd be wrong. Bring on Krzysztof, a slightly ethereal figure who floats into my room at intervals throughout each night. It is the job of this gentle Polish man to measure, examine, siphon, record and remove the necessities of my bodily output.

During these otherwise pleasure-less exercises, we talk about Krzysztof's favourite director and fellow Pole, Roman

Polanski, and of his extraordinary, murky cinematic output and life story. It's a wonderful distraction from the dubious task in hand. We start with Roman's student short film *Two Men and a Wardrobe* (1958) and his debut feature *Knife in the Water* (1962). Then we proceed through many of the other thirty-six films he has directed. Krzysztof comes alive at the mention of Polanski's *Rosemary's Baby* (1968), *Chinatown* (1974), *Tess* (1979), *Frantic* (1988) and *The Pianist* (2002). But my drainage technician always returns to his unhealthy addiction to the torrid affairs between cruise-ship passengers in *Bitter Moon* (1992). Fortunately, he studiously avoids bringing up Roman Polanski's personal experiences with Nazis, assassins, the Charles Manson Gang, his criminal conviction for statutory rape, brief prison time and subsequent escape to non-extraditable France. Krzysztof knows that I have enough minor demons of my own to deal with.

If at night I am a film student, then during the day I'm concentrating on my physical education. I am convinced that this is the secret to my own escape. I tuck my iPhone into the pocket of my dressing gown and head off, very unsteadily at first, to patrol the corridors between the wards. An app on the phone shows me the distance that I've travelled each day. One time, I clock up in excess of two kilometres, which is a lot of disinfectant-smelling hospital passages to have navigated. The other advantage of these sorties is that I get to meet a range of medics, as well as other bruised and broken inmates.

Sometimes I'll bump into a young surgical assistant, who will give me some gossip about my own procedure, or details of the most recent cutting they have been involved in. On other occasions, I'll chat with a patient who has also had the idea of starting a pedestrian right-of-way. We discuss our best routes, shortcuts and most-favoured toilets. Every adventure involves encouragement and cheery jokes from passing nurses, and always a chance to hustle more painkillers from them. If I'm very lucky, I'll meet the consultant boss man himself, Sean Martin, and I can impress him with my strength, agility and mental prowess.

Sure, I'll be out of here in no time.

Not so fast.

I am moved in with some fellow VRE-infected patients. Losing my single room to a larger ward full of enforced relationships, with a random collection of hard cases, is always a jolt. But I am relatively lucky again this time. Next to me, I have a young, tattooed Corkman, with a mild demeanour and a great sense of humour. Which is just as well, because all is not plain sailing. The output from my operation-site drain looks suspiciously like urine, in which case my bladder hasn't sealed or healed. This is making the ever-watchful Sean Martin worried and unhappy. The dubious output from my stoma leaks onto my surgical wound and starts to cause an infection. Then shock, horror, another weekend has arrived, and you now know what that means in hospital life: the dreaded skeleton crew of nurses and reduced dose of doctors.

The nurses are under particular pressure, as managers move them between wards and shifts, with students and agency substitutes filling in the gaps. I notice that staffing levels have deteriorated, even in the short six months since I was last on a post-surgical ward. A senior nurse, whose talent and confidence I immediately sense with relief, suddenly disappears late one evening. The next day, I ask her what happened. She tells me that she was sent to help a newly qualified nurse, on her first day in the job, who had been put in charge of the overflow ward from A&E. She had eighteen patients on her own, one of whom she thought was going to die during the overnight shift. She was, naturally, vulnerable and terrified, and did the right thing by calling for reinforcements. Nevertheless, that situation definitely left a nursing gap on our ward.

On another occasion, I meet a uniformed nurse who tells me that she is actually a pharmacist now, but has returned to the ward to help out, and freely admits that it's difficult to remember how everything works. It is all hands on deck in this over-stressed environment and the nurses are struggling to keep on top of it all. We patients can only feel sorry for them all, in this austerity situation that is not of their making.

We also latch onto our favourites and word quickly goes around as to which students are naturally talented and which are struggling. We would be good academic examiners, here on the front line, if only anyone bothered to ask.

Numbers of staff become especially depleted on Sunday afternoon. A posse of us goes on an expedition, roaming the corridors to kidnap a rare nurse and bring her back to one of our distressed ward-mates.

Tattooed Corkman and I arrive at Monday morning with a sense of relief. We are both ready and waiting with our moans and complaints for the senior doctors, when they come on their rounds: he has painful water retention in his privates, and I need my septic surgical wound to be lanced. We're still in the proverbial wars.

Although the very considerable number of medics in my life at this moment would hate to hear me say this, one of my saving graces is that I am still taking the opiate combinations of long-lasting OxyContin and quick-relief OxyNorm. Even though I am on low doses, these morphine-based drugs are highly addictive and can cause big problems for people who are prescribed higher quantities. I have now been taking the daily opiates for a period of six months, which is definitely frowned on by the medical establishment.

But here is my argument in favour, followed by my own caveats and warnings. In addition to dulling the physical post-operative pain, I believe that the Oxys have been instrumental in maintaining my mental health up to this point. I have a serious disease and the realisation of that fact frequently occurs to my consciousness with a surreal and unpalatable aftertaste. The Oxys allow me to face the day in the morning and give me a definite, always appreciated 'upper' amid the exhaustion of the evenings. Without them I would have found the whole experience much harder to deal with psychologically, and for that I am grateful.

Three months after this second major operation, when it is simply becoming embarrassing that I am still taking the Oxys, my family doctor and first saviour, Ed McSwiney, gives me an ultimatum (or rather refuses to give me another prescription) and we agree to go cold turkey. I have three weeks of withdrawal symptoms that consist of 'the shakes' in bed at night and generally heightened grumpiness during the day. I watch a documentary on television, outlining the dangers of transition from doctor-prescribed higher doses of the Oxys to illicit 'hard drugs', as illustrated by a horrific epidemic in certain states in America. I am happy that I am not dealing with that trauma and wouldn't wish it on my worst enemy. But I also have to be honest about the physical and psychological benefits of the Oxys. In the correctly prescribed low doses, they have definitely helped me through my long and sometimes difficult struggle.

On a lighter note – albeit of darker humour – there is an occasion when my knowledge of OxyNorm gives me a really good laugh. If you've been on the combination of the Oxys for as long as I have, then there's a law of diminishing returns:

the immediate physical effects are much lower in strength, sometimes almost unnoticeable. You forget how powerful the damn things were in the first throes of post-operative pain. During the anxiety of this latest weekend in The Hospital, I suggest to the tattooed Corkman that he asks the nurses for an OxyNorm tablet, to ease his considerable distress and discomfort in the nether region. A junior doctor approves the request and Cork swallows the pill. After a while, he gets out of bed and begins to drift around the ward in a state of pain-relieved ecstasy and spiritual transcendence. Then he roars over to me in his broader-than-usual accent:

'Sure, no wonder you love these things so much. Look at the state of me! I'm off my bleeding head, boy!'

I'm not laughing, however, when I have to visit the bladder-testing unit, or whatever its official title is. My porter-powered trolley leaves the ward, winding along familiar corridors and down several storeys in the elevator. The young doctor with the handbag and golden chain is waiting for me, ready for action once more, in the company of another nurse. After our last encounter, my confidence ebbs away, as it seems to me that she is not very experienced. Her job this time is to flood my recently re-sealed bladder with liquid, then scan it and store the photographs, so that the surgeons can ascertain whether it has healed or not. The liquid goes in through my penis too fast, and very painfully, so the nurse stops the flow. Some images are taken, and I politely decline the request to proceed to a full tank for further photographic evidence. I've had enough, and I need to protect my lovely new bladder, even if the scan shows that it is wildly misshapen, like a distorted balloon.

Back on the ward, one of the more junior nurses is given the tricky task of withdrawing the main drain from my surgical site. She starts to pull on the large tube but it gets stuck at the exit wound. I'm expecting her to halt. Instead, she gives it a sharp, painful tug. Out it comes, followed by a lot more liquid than she was clearly expecting. My bed is awash with a far from pretty red sea.

***

Finally, proceedings turn the corner and all gets better. A doctor sets up a makeshift operating theatre on the ward and successfully lances my infected wound. Sean Martin arrives with news from the laboratory that there is no trace of urine in the drain from the operation site, a matter of professional satisfaction to him for a job well done, and of great personal relief to me.

This sense of optimism and well-being rises through the roof when Anne White enters with my pathology results. They show that not one of the many lymph nodes that were extracted has any trace of cancerous cells. This is a very important milestone. Deirdre and I shed a tear or three. Anne gives us an emotional smile also. I am acutely aware that, for every one of her cases where good news is imparted, she has to experience the ordeal of bringing disappointment or even devastation to another patient.

I leave The Hospital twelve days after the operation. Christmas is in sight. I will have the catheter attached to me until a few days beforehand. This means managing bags of pee, day and night, everywhere I go. I don't realise at this moment that, as Deirdre has been told, there is a possibility I may have to do this for all my days.

I arrive back at The Hospital three weeks after my discharge, on 23 December, to have the catheter removed. It's a weird and uncomfortable feeling as the tube slithers from my most private innards. But this is another step towards freedom, as far as I am concerned, so I grin and bear it. The nurse who takes it out warns me that, if I can't urinate in the next couple of hours, she will have to put the catheter back in. No chance, I think to myself.

I haunt the corridors of The Hospital once more, and drink bottles of water to get everything flowing. Then it's time to relieve myself, which I successfully do, amid a bit of blood and pain, but who the hell cares about that at this stage? I never thought that I'd be saying this, but my most magnificent Christmas present this year, courtesy of Santa Claus Sean Martin (who must have received my letter in time), is a miraculous, perfectly working, refashioned bladder, sans catheter, and a potentially cancer-free body.

Tattooed Corkman and I finally perfect our escape. We wish each other Seasons Greetings and speed away on our sleighs, travelling in different directions across the powdery snow, to fresh and hope-filled horizons.

BEATLING

It was time to become a true Beatlemaniac.

I knew that, if I were to do justice to the editing and curation of Sir George Martin's definitive autobiography, my levels of familiarity with both George's life and all things Beatles would have to be set high. The amount written, recorded and filmed about The Beatles alone represents its own mountain of appropriately Himalayan proportions. But their producer's life and work before, during and after his involvement with that world-famous band is its own rich and astonishing story. It was my aim, during the research for and assembly of George Martin's book, to become a useful promoter of the work when publication time arrived, even in the face of the most ardent and knowledgeable fans. I had about three years to achieve that usefulness. This was just the beginning.

I started reading multiple volumes about The Beatles, watched their own films and the documentaries about them. I also listened to all of the music, of course, in its many different versions and mixes. I simultaneously enjoyed delving into George Martin's world. There were myriad books, articles, television programmes and radio profiles about him too.

These included the most recent screen documentary, *Produced by George Martin* (dir. Francis Hanly, 2011). That was the *BBC Arena* portrait that had convinced me to ask George to play a role in my ultimately ill-fated wartime film, *Wayfaring Strangers*. I saw immediately from the documentary that he had always been very comfortable and charismatic in front of the cameras, in footage of him captured across five decades.

When George Martin died in March 2016, at the age of ninety, Paul McCartney wrote of him on his website: 'If anyone earned the title of the fifth Beatle it was George. From the day that he gave The Beatles our first recording contract, to the last time I saw him, he was the most generous, intelligent and musical person I've ever had the pleasure to know.'[1]

Now it was my job to recapture the essence of that brilliant person, by editing his three autobiographical books. This task was made even more daunting and exciting by a new development on the original brief. I could also research and include other public domain material either written by George, or recorded in interviews with him. In addition, there was the tantalising prospect of being given access to previously unpublished private and personal writings that would be provided by the Martin family. Undoubtedly, it was this latter promise, as well as the never-ending thirst for everything Beatles-related, that would drive book sales and

1   Paul McCartney's website: www.paulmccartney.com/news-blogs/news/paul-mccartney-on-george-martin.

public interest. But I felt that one of the most exciting aspects of the journey would be the recalibrating of the relationship between the most famous juncture of George's life – signing and producing The Beatles – and Martin's other private and personal achievements, which would have been called a huge success in anyone else's life story.

He had come from a very poor London family, taught himself to play the piano as a child and trained in the Fleet Air Arm of the Royal Navy during the Second World War. He connected with a 'fairy godfather by post' when he started a correspondence with Sidney Harrison, a man who secured him not only a classical music education at the Guildhall School of Music and Drama, but also a follow-up job at Abbey Road Studios in 1950. As George himself wrote: 'That's where I was lucky. That's where God's timing for me was absolutely right.'[2]

Within five years he was made boss of the Parlophone recording label. In a move of some courage, and amid ridicule from other colleagues at the parent company EMI, he added comedy records to the exclusively classical output for which his label was more renowned. George boosted the careers of Spike Milligan, Peter Sellers, Beyond the Fringe and many more, almost single-handedly starting the phenomenon of comedy and novelty records climbing into the hit parade.

---

2   Martin, George and Hornsby, Jeremy, *All You Need Is Ears* (St Martin's Press, New York, 1979), p. 10.

Notoriously, The Beatles had been turned down by every other major record label in London, and George himself was less than enamoured by their demo recordings when he first heard them in the company of their manager, Brian Epstein. But when he actually met 'the Boys', George loved their charismatic energy and, having decided to sign The Beatles, he always stressed his uncanny good fortune in stumbling upon a group of the greatest songwriters and performers of all time. For his part, Martin revolutionised the creative input that a producer brings to music recording and his classical background was a crucial influence in that mix.

Once The Beatles had disbanded, George kept up a phenomenally productive output. He built AIR studios in London and the West Indies, attracting his own Who's Who of internationally renowned artistes over four decades. He wrote movie scores and travelled the world, conducting orchestras and staging shows, while never neglecting his interest in the offbeat or unusual.

Late in life, George started to become profoundly deaf and handed the baton over to his son, Giles. They worked together as joint musical directors on George's last hurrah, The Beatles *LOVE* show in Las Vegas, for which he won his sixth Grammy at the age of eighty-two.

George had told me about his own illness, and I also knew that he had started an annual event called *Sound and Vision* at Abbey Road Studios, raising over £1.5 million in aid of Cancer

Research UK. Those facts meant a lot to me, personally, and were an ongoing inspiration as I attempted to honour the life of a man who was widely respected and admired, and not just by Beatlemaniacs.

WEDNESDAY, 4 JANUARY 2017

Having bid a strong 'goodbye and good riddance' to the year of 2016, I resume my visits to The Hospital, with a New Year spring in my step.

I'm in for a shock. Or two.

This time I need to have stents removed from the ureter tubes that lead between my kidneys and bladder. They were inserted during the last operation, in November, and it's time for them to come out. This procedure is called a flexible cystoscopy and it only takes a few minutes. There will be no anaesthetic administered, before the tiny camera and grabbing utensil (probably not the technical term) are pushed up inside my penis and into the bladder. Each stent is a piece of plastic tubing about eight inches long with a curled, bendy hook on the end to keep it in position.

As the first one is captured and dragged from within me, I can't believe the level of pain. It's unlike anything I have ever known. As he expertly goes in for the second stent, the attending doctor blithely asks me if I would like to watch the procedure on the digital screen nearby. Apart from the fact that I am temporarily unable to speak, I can't look at the screen because I need to keep my eyes closed and concentrate on my iron grip of the metal bars at the sides of the bed. I am cruciform, as I grit my teeth for the other half of the ordeal. I suddenly can't help thinking that my original next-door patient, Rose, would have been suitably impressed by my suffering.

I survive. Just. When I get home, I am inspired to go on my first in-depth medical Google search since the beginning of this journey. I am determined to find out what other patients around the World Wide Web have made of this method of torture. Perhaps I am just a complete wimp? Apparently not.

A grimacing smile of recognition crosses my face as I read the words of an American paratrooper, on an Internet messaging board: 'I fought in Vietnam in the 1970s. On different occasions, I was both shot and stabbed. Neither event was as painful as the hospital procedure I have recently undergone, which is called a flexible cystoscopy.'

I unashamedly award myself a medal of valour following that particular Battle of Treatment Hill. Another of our boxes has been ticked. The destination is alluring to us now. The ending is in sight. And it is seemingly a happy, Hollywood-type one. If we are to fully embrace the cliché, as earlier promised, then we can see the bright exit from the tunnel ahead. Our blessings are being counted hard.

Later in the month, I am sent for a high-tech positron emission tomography (PET) scan, which is only available at a local private hospital. Thankfully, I am able to avail of it, even as a public patient. It is provided to me, free of charge, by the unheralded Irish taxpayer. Radioactive liquid glucose is pumped into one of my veins and allowed time to circulate around my body. Most cancers will synthesise the glucose faster than normal cells and will therefore show up on the scan as unwelcome hotspots of activity. It's a brilliant technology, but a little unnerving to undergo because there's no hiding from the accuracy of these results. The technician gives nothing away on the day, apart from asking me to avoid contact with pregnant women because I will remain aglow with potentially damaging radioactivity for several hours. I promise to do my best.

Within the week, we are back in David Fennelly's office. The results of the PET scan seem magnificently clear of cancer. There is a small patch of 'uptake' that the analysts are putting down to an active area of post-operative healing. No one seems worried by it. I am grateful to David for getting me access to the PET scan. The results have given me huge peace of mind.

But there is also a serious conversation to be had. Increasingly, now that the treatment is going well, we are being told, and also admitting to ourselves, just how troubling the prognosis was at the beginning. We need to consider that the risks of recurrence extend into the future. For this reason, Dr Fennelly feels that additional chemotherapy and immunotherapy would be advisable, to give me the best chances for survival in the longer term. He is backed up in this conclusion by the rest of my medical team.

Again, I choose not to ask for the statistical analysis: what percentage of this and how many years of that? I'm not in any way judging the many patients who want or need their doctors to break their journeys down into mathematical norms or expectations, and who find sanity and solace in doing so. However, I discover that I don't. That's also a complimentary reflection of the trust I am able to place in the people who have saved my life. To have landed in on top of them in The Hospital, by the skin of my teeth in terms of geography and timing, has been my great good fortune. For now, I am cancer free. I could decline David Fennelly's offer of more treatment. But I'd be a fool to do so.

Instead, I have to gird my loins to meet a new chemotherapy combination called FOLFIRI, with a fresh selection of side effects. I also have to embrace once more my old friend Erbitux, the immunotherapy drug with its delightful skin rash. I will have to learn to manage all of this, with the extra demands of the stoma bag. Since one of the glorious gifts bestowed by my new chemotherapy will be regular diarrhoea, proximity to sanitary facilities will become more than a minor obsession.

So I am strapping in for another three months of downhill travel, temporarily and voluntarily eschewing wellness for illness. Here goes.

On the first day of my new cycle of drugs, in darkest February, I am emotional and a little downhearted. Still very thin, I have some dull pain in my bones that is making me anxious, in spite of the encouraging PET scan results. Overall, my weight has dropped from thirteen-and-a-half stone (or eighty-six kilos) to nine stone (or fifty-seven kilos). Under these circumstances I become much more aware of my actual skeleton. It's painful to sit down when my natural buttock cushion has disappeared. All aches and sores become worrisome to the paranoid brain inside my skull.

Suzie delivers me to and from The Hospital session, which is as comforting as usual. However, in my darker moments, I feel like this ordeal will go on and on: that I won't ever rise up again, to the strong and healthy state that I was previously in before my cancer took hold.

Once more I can feel the toxic, life-saving substances coursing through my blood as I am flooded with them over a six-hour period by the experienced nurses on the ward. Yet again, the portacath device implanted under my skin allows for easy transfusion of the drugs, entering as they do through a plastic vein sitting prominently across the top of my hard, protruding collarbone.

While my final session of the first course of chemotherapy was conducted in mid-summer sun, this time a blue, chilly, mid-winter moon shines outside. The nurses marvel at it through the windows, when they finally disconnect my intravenous tubes at day's end. They send me away from the day ward with my regular little present, suspended on a belt around my waist: it's a plastic orb called a bolus, containing a balloon full of additional chemotherapy drugs. These will slowly release into my system over the next forty-eight hours, just in case I might be in danger of getting a bit too cocky or pleased with myself. I am given a kit to have on standby, in the event that I ever have to clear up a spillage. It contains protective eye goggles, a plastic cape and rubber gloves. Fortunately, I never have to use it.

I retreat homewards to the warmth of my bed, and the reward of Deirdre and the children fussing around me with tea, toast and hugs. I feel poisoned again already, even after session one. My body immediately recognises the onslaught. And the bolus keeps topping me up.

While the delirious doldrums begin to set in, I think to myself that I'd love some celestial encouragement to help me through. Some of us look for, and find, signposts and signals as we wander through life. Other people call them coincidences. I'm looking for one now, to kick-start my energies once more, inspiring me further along this meandering road that belongs only to *The Fighting Man*.

As I languish beneath the bed covers, I fire up my laptop computer. I start scrolling through the bookmarks at the top of my Firefox. ('Firefox sake!' I can't help my brain thinking.) Suddenly, Cillian Murphy's face stares up at me from the homepage of an Irish news website. I am immediately intrigued. Deirdre and I had dinner with Cillian and his wife, Yvonne, only three weeks ago.

Our mutual friends, actor Mikel Murfi and radio producer Eithne Hand, had created an amazing tasting menu of twelve delicious courses, each served to the strains of particular pieces of music, with a printed explanation of their culinary and aural significances. All this was delivered with a dollop of Mikel and Eithne's uniquely anarchic sense of humour and theatrical fun. It was one of the highlights of the New Year period, and the first time we were out with friends in over nine months. It was a special gift for us.

Now I double-click unceremoniously on the centre of Cillian's face. A music video starts to play. In it, he drives a car through eerie night scenes, to the strains of a new song by Irish singer-songwriter Fionn Regan. It's called 'The Meetings of the Waters' and, after the day I've had on the cancer treatment ward, the spirit of the song speaks directly to my wallowing self. With descriptions that are uncannily familiar to me, Fionn's beautifully haunting voice assures me that my ordeal will not go on and on, and that I will rise up once more. He tells me that the light from the moon is going to shine down on my collarbone and fix all my ailments. I may have been hollowed out, the song suggests, but my power to revive myself has not disappeared.

I play this inspirational music many times over. Later,

I write all of the lyrics out on a page and seal them in an envelope. Paki Smith, the painter of *The Fighting Man*, flies across the world and floats them down the Ganges for me, in the time-honoured practice of Hindu offerings on India's holiest river.

He just happens to be going in that direction.

CRACKING

It has always been difficult for the actual month-by-month, year-on-year process of developing a screenplay to possess a sense of entertaining drama in itself. It has remained even more difficult to try to report on the process of developing a screenplay, draft after draft, with even a hint of the excitement that a car chase would bring. Compared to an action set piece, screenwriting has forever been long, laborious and intermittently tedious. But, in the case of *The Safe*, one aspect of it was consistently interesting: the screenwriter.

While we were in the middle of our own development process on that film, I went to see a performance by Owen O'Neill of his new one-man play: *Ten Songs to Die For.* He was touring it around Ireland, after a hectic month-long run at the Edinburgh Festival. The storytelling was craftily intercut with a careful selection of music tracks, hence the title. Each song related to an astonishing event in Owen's past and present family life. No spoilers here. Except to say that the play possessed the same attributes that his other dramas have always had a reputation for: strong, searingly honest and personal tales, caressing and accosting their audiences with both comedy and pathos. This combination has ever been the finest of lines, and it's one that we were trying to walk again with our collaboration on *The Safe*.

I loved the opening premise of his screenplay from the first time I read it. It is set in County Kerry in 2008, exactly at the time of the Irish banking crash and the infamous government bailout. In Owen's story, Enda runs a local garage business with his adult son, Harry. In light of recent events, Enda decides on his own dramatic course of action. He takes their life savings out of the bank in bundles of cash and locks them into an old American safe that he has bought for the purpose. He then loses the numbers to the combination lock.

That delicious conundrum was established less than five minutes into the proposed film. But, of course, the real stories and themes then kicked in. They were full of character conflicts and historical family complications, all the intriguing additional layers that Owen's skilful storytelling and darkly comic timing brought to the script.

We needed to interrogate, dissect, improve and embroider every aspect of the story and screenplay. That was the job in hand. But, as director and part-producer, I wasn't working in any form of a vacuum here; Owen knew his way around the process. For example, purely through the quality of his speculative writing, my collaborator had persuaded Stephen King to grant him the stage adaptation rights to one of the maestro's most treasured novellas, and the cinematic classic that had already sprung from it: *The Shawshank Redemption*. Owen's theatrical version had been successfully touring for several years in Britain and was due to expand further, to Kansas and beyond, during the upcoming year.

Nevertheless, we still had to find our own way of working and colluding together. It was vital to discover whether our ideas, suggestions and notes, on successive and continuing drafts of the script, truly and honestly gelled. Owen wrote fast and was willing to respond quickly to my feedback. That was a huge help to our momentum. We had managed to attract some development funding, but there was a lot of legal and administrative work needed before hard cash could be unlocked from the funder's safe. All of that took me several months to complete. It helped that Owen was prepared to continue to commit to the screenplay during this time. I felt that he was improving *The Safe* with each pass. So did he. That is an essential test for continued belief in the development of a story or script. It is possible to take backward steps or blind alleys and still succeed, but you don't want too many of them. They sap the energy out of the long exercise.

As the screenplay progressed, we were inevitably thinking about favourite actors to fill the roles, no matter how far into the future that might be. Attracting sought-after actors is a tricky business: they have plenty of roles to choose from; they need to be reassured by the quality of cast and crew that will be around them, and on whom their best performance will depend; they must also be available, obviously, in terms of their busy schedules; and, completing a non-exclusive list, their role needs to have enough 'moments' for them to be tempted by it. I think my wife coined that word, being an actress herself, but also having been the casting director on two feature films many moons ago. She underlined the truism that an actor is always looking for a role that has enough depth, some unique quality, a strong overall pull on the story, and a good quota of dramatic 'moments' that stand out for the audience and provide satisfaction for the performer.

Enda and Harry, father and son, needed to have equally strong stories for the film to work and also to attract the actors we wanted. On this latest draft of the script I had the feeling that the father's journey was getting really strong. Above all, there was an ending to it that was right on the money, forgiving the pun. But the character of Harry, and the actor who would play him, needed something on a par, and that was a tough call to demand of the screenwriter. I laid down the challenge and received a response by way of an amended script.

I read it with trepidation, suspecting that I would probably have to let Owen down gently, and suggest that we need to think again. What I didn't expect was to be made to laugh, in a scene of emotional turmoil, as the writer caressed and accosted me with both comedy and pathos.

He had walked that fine line brilliantly.
It was definitely a 'moment'.

FRIDAY, 17 FEBRUARY 2017

I've had longish hair for twenty-five years now, since before Deirdre met me. It's been going grey, admittedly, but has remained a prominent feature, part of my delusional Samson complex.

Now, as I start to wrestle with bouts of a different chemotherapy combination, I sit down in a hairdresser's chair, ready to be shorn. Marie O'Brien, the oncology nurse who works closely with David Fennelly, has warned me that my hair will soon start to come out in clumps. It's an additional side effect of the new FOLFIRI drug regime that I am undergoing. I'm not destined to be shiny bald, Marie says, but I will start moulting heavily. She advises that the easiest way to lessen the physical and psychological impact is to get out the shears.

It's a small price to pay. I am aware of how much this past year has made me revert to a childish state, dependent on the decisions and support of others. Somewhat surprisingly, it has happened without embarrassment. I have embraced my vulnerability willingly. I conclude that it's part of the healing process, this temporary retreat from adult egotism.

The altered state doesn't diminish my sense of determination and resilience. If anything, it unexpectedly facilitates the fight. Other people support me in this regression, shouldering my responsibilities and relieving my anxieties.

I have to admit, if reluctantly, that I'm getting more adventurous with Google now. As the sessions of chemotherapy and immunotherapy progress, I read the printed dosages on the bags of liquid that are waiting to seep through my veins. Their garish green and purple poison-warnings hang ominously on a rail above me. As far as I can discern from my Internet research, Dr Fennelly is giving me the highest possible transfusions of both the FOLFIRI and the repeat immunotherapy, Erbitux. This will give me the best chance to benefit from them. But I also know that I have to prepare myself for the rough and tumble of the unavoidable consequences of such a high dosage. Or, as my oncologist himself says, with honesty: 'I'm going to make you very ill.'

I enter into a distinct physical cycle every time I have to take the drugs. It begins with a woozy, unsteady feeling during the liquid chemical invasion of my body on the long day of transfusion. This effect would be worse if I wasn't being administered an allergy-preventing antihistamine, in the form of intravenous Piriton, and an anti-diarrhoea drug called Atropine, which is injected into the stomach wall and feels like a bad wasp sting. There follows two manageable days when the hospital-administered steroids and the twice-daily oral Dexamethasone keep the body and soul energised. Then there's a week of shit. Chronic fatigue alongside sapping stomach runs, cracking skin on the feet, a mountainous rash on the torso and face, topped off with split nails and a sore mouth. After which, it's almost time to begin the next cycle.

I visit my original hero and local doctor, Ed McSwiney, and he gives me the antibiotic minocycline. It starts to lessen the grating effect of the rash. Several layers of skin have already been stripped away by now. When it is healed by this new medicine, the surface of my face suddenly looks smooth and fresh. Suzie tells me that a lot of people would pay a lot of money for a facial peel as good as that.

As part of my routine, I venture into The Hospital the day before each cycle of drugs. Even though I have a portacath, I still have to visit the phlebotomy department to give a regular blood sample from a vein in my arms. I'm usually well enough to take a train there and back. I feel like a school child using public transport for the first time. This is the greatest modicum of solo freedom I've had for nearly a year. I already feel like a veteran of the cancer war, and so do my arms. The veins have receded inwards and it's hard for the phlebotomists to find one. I can gauge their level of experience and expertise by how quickly they do so, or by how many tries it takes. If the results of the blood tests are 'good' when they come back from the laboratory, then the treatment is given the go ahead.

If I'm neutropenic, with dangerously low white cells, then everything grinds to a halt. This happens on cycle three, and I have to take an enforced week-long break from the regime. I know I'm properly toxic, because my energy levels have tumbled drastically. I succumb to the reality of having to wait out these cold months before I feel well again.

But, believe me, I'm also actively planning my escape from this illness and this treatment. I am focusing on far-off hills and I'm making travel plans for how to reach them. In the meantime, I have the luxury of a snug home, and a wife who is working like a dervish to keep us afloat financially, with generous help from family and friends. The children are happy in their now-not-so-new school and we have found a real-life Mary Poppins called Samantha, whom they adore.

While the tiredness flattens me into the bed, the freshly rediscovered medium of the radio raises me up. My nightly fix, now that the morphine of the Oxys has been so rudely taken from me, is provided by John Creedon, between eight o'clock and ten on RTÉ, followed by Tom Dunne, for two more hours, on Newstalk. Their selections and knowledge of music are constantly inspiring and uplifting. These are the apparently small, but really very important, experiences that help to keep a patient with a long-term illness motivated. I thank them both for hundreds of hours of happy distraction.

The West Brit in me has to pay attention to what is being said in the media on the other side of the Irish Sea. I haven't yet managed to break that bond, despite my grateful return to the bosom of Mother Ireland.

Some months before this second period of my chemotherapy treatment, I started to listen to the 'cancer diary' of British journalist Steve Hewlett, and I continue to follow it now. It plays every Monday, shortly after five o'clock, on BBC Radio 4. Steve was diagnosed at the same time as I was. He was told that he had oesophageal cancer that had metastasised to his liver. He has bravely decided to broadcast a weekly report on his progress. As a seasoned radio and television journalist who anchors *The Media Show*, Steve has taken a completely different approach to mine. He has researched his condition meticulously, studying best practices in treatment, possible clinical trials, options that are available to him on the NHS, and others outside of that system, which he can pay for privately.

As the weekly airing gathers momentum, Steve's courageous radio diary stirs up a considerable audience response. People agree with his contention that the subject of cancer needs to be spoken about more openly, so that the millions who are affected by it can share and learn from their joint experiences. I immediately relate to so much of what Steve says, and I appreciate his barefaced honesty. He provides articulate descriptions of what it is like to be diagnosed, the difficulties of undergoing chemotherapy, the physical pain of weight loss, the struggles with dehydration, and the strange but not necessarily morbid or unpleasant fascination that we patients develop with aspects of our bodies while moving through the process of treatment and change. Steve eloquently outlines the ups and downs of his own case. He describes the side effects that cause delays to his treatment, and the anxious thoughts of what the cancer is doing inside him during these periods, when not being attacked by the medics and medicines. Most of the time he is unerringly optimistic and good-natured. He's a kindred spirit.

Steve also discusses *The Sunday Times* newspaper accounts of his more famous journalistic colleague, A. A. Gill, which are running concurrently, just as their cancers are. Gill described himself on first diagnosis as having 'an embarrassment of cancer, the full English'.[1] He also documents and laments the fact that, under NHS guidelines, he has not qualified for an immunotherapy drug called Nivolumab. In his own infamously combative A. A. Gill style, he describes asking his doctor why the NHS has one of the worst outcomes for cancer treatment in the whole of Europe.[2]

Steve Hewlett captures his audience's attention with a ticking clock narrative of what he feels is a vital part of his own treatment: getting access to the very latest immunotherapy drugs. Steve decides to pay for a drug called Ramucirumab, on top of the chemotherapy drugs the NHS is already

1   *The Sunday Times*, 20 November 2016.
2   *Ibid.*, 11 December 2016.

administering to him. This will cost £12,724 for four cycles of the treatment. A sum that is much less, Steve tells us with amusement, than it would have been before he lost so much body weight due to his illness, because kilograms are the yardstick of the monetary calculation for the drug.

A. A. Gill dies on 10 December 2016, three months after his initial diagnosis. Steve Hewlett is clearly taken aback in his weekly broadcast. As are we, his audience. Then he charges on, unbowed, through Christmas and the New Year. There are a couple of audio diary entries that describe setbacks requiring hospital stays. But he also lifts the mood with the optimistic news of his qualification, at the very last minute, for a clinical trial of the immunotherapy treatment Nivolumab. This was the drug that Gill wasn't entitled to receive under NHS guidelines until it was too late. Steve describes his tears of relief on discovering that he has gained access to the international trial. Audience members express their appreciation in waves of emails and texts to the programme's producers. I also cling vicariously to Steve's journey, empathising in a way that I could never have done before the onset of my own illness.

Then, in the very next weekly episode, comes a thunderbolt that all cancer patients fear and push to the back of their minds. Steve Hewlett relays the details with extraordinary dignity, strength and grace. His thoughts seem to be only for the welfare of those around him. He tells us that he has just married his partner, after doctors informed him that his liver is no longer able to break down the drugs. They have told him that all treatment, apart from palliative care, must stop. Steve says that he has 'weeks, possibly months'. As it transpires, it is the last time we hear his warm, articulate, cancer-rattled voice.

Steve's death on 20 February 2017 has a profound effect on me, and on many of his other radio listeners, judging by their response. I am in the middle of receiving chemotherapy and immunotherapy when I hear the news. Apart from my sense of sadness for Steve and his family, two things immediately occur to me.

First, how incredibly lucky I have been in my treatment as a public patient in the Republic of Ireland, particularly in the receipt of the immunotherapy drug Erbitux, also known as Cetuximab. The 'mab', as Steve Hewlett has educated his audience, standing for 'monoclonal antibody'. I have also been on the sharp receiving end of two surgeons who, as my oncologist David Fennelly impresses upon me, are so expert that they could work in any centre of medical excellence any-where in the world. But, to continue misquoting Humphrey Bogart, they just so happen to work in mine. Through those consultants' expertise, and the brilliantly prescribed start to the whole process that I was given by gastroenterologist Juliette Sheridan, I have been blessed with a chance to beat the odds (I know that much about the numbers), and my body's response to their surgery and medicines has been exceptional. Like any film director worth his or her salt, I should at least try to take the credit for other people's excellent work, and for the hand played by Lady Luck (as well as any other mysterious intercessions that may have occurred). But, in good conscience, I really and truly can't.

Second, that of all the many cancer patients I have sat next to for long hours on the chemotherapy day ward of The Hospital, not a single one has approached their treatment and condition with anything but grit, determination and expressions of support for their fellow travellers. This camaraderie is a weird and wonderful thing to behold, under the circumstances. I salute the late Steve Hewlett for having carried on that tradition to the very end.

Now, it's time for some comedy.

Seriously.

Deirdre has decided that, not having enough to deal with in her own busy and rather fraught life, she needs to do something practical to help a few others. In particular, some of the refugees who have been pouring across European borders as the result of conflicts in Syria and elsewhere, as well as people here in Ireland who are suffering under a worsening homelessness crisis. In cooperation with television producer Darren Smith and manager Jane Russell, she is mounting the biggest stand-up comedy gig that Ireland has ever seen: *Paddy's Night in Support of Comic Relief.*

A list of top Irish comedians, willing to give their services free gratis, soon fills the 3Arena in Dublin with 8,000 avid comedy fans. On this one night together, they raise the impressive sum of €200,000 to help a range of needy charities. It is the best comedy gig I have ever seen, and I have attended a few in my time. I am more than a little proud of my wonderful missus. And also of myself: just for bloody well being there to tell the tale.

HUSBANDING

I need to talk more about Deirdre.

Deirdre O'Kane and I first met when we moved in next door to each other, in the historic but dilapidated area of Ireland's capital city known as the Liberties. Three guys lived beside three girls, even before that famous American television show had been invented. Eventually, two couples coupled. One survived. Us. Deirdre was beautiful, sexy, strong-willed, exciting and adventurous. I had initially avoided her as much as possible for two whole years, in an attempt to stay out of trouble. Then came one of those unpredictable moments when two people fall passionately, achingly in love and they know that their lives will always be inextricably linked. There was a magical freedom to it. We rented a small garden flat on picturesque Dartmouth Square and lived together pretty blissfully as our careers started to gain some traction.

Now, exactly a quarter of a century later, Deirdre deserved something by way of a reward after all these tough times, which actually stretched back beyond my illness, to the years of trying to push *Noble* up that unforgiving distribution hill. The film had been Deirdre's passion project since she first read

Christina Noble's books, two decades ago. As much as anyone else involved, and not just because she was playing the leading role, she wanted that film to fly further than it did. Most of all, she desired it for Christina herself, who undoubtedly merited wider international recognition and, perhaps as a concomitant result of the film's release, could have found new support for the never-ending financial burden of keeping her children's foundation going in Vietnam, Mongolia and elsewhere. The middle road that the film settled into was a hard one for Deirdre's dreams to take. Indeed, all the major participants in the project had some readjusting to undergo, after the dust had settled.

So, by 2018, we had largely come to terms with that final state of affairs, certainly after what had then happened to my health. But I was always waiting and hoping for Deirdre's next big opportunity to appear. Then, suddenly it did, with the chance of a role that she would have loved to capture. In typical style, Deirdre began to fight hard to make it happen. A whirlwind surrounded her, and enveloped our household, as she started to put in the work and energy that was needed in order to succeed. She put all her focus on the line, and I waited with bated breath to see what would happen.

As a background to this moment, I should explain that in the past Deirdre and I have often worked together, at intervals. We can't help it. When she was writing her latest stand-up show, *A Line of O'Kane,* I would type up the script and finesse the structure and the jokes with her, sitting on a couch in the window of our favourite coffee shop, Leonardo's. For bread and butter jobs, we would pen radio commercials, or devise tailor-made comedy sets for corporate events and television slots. With optimistic hopes, we had recently made the pilot for *The Deirdre O'Kane Show*. All the screenplays that I have ever written have been the subject of hours and hours of conversation between the two of us. Deirdre has always been my first and then my final reader.

I've often teased my wife when she has dismissed one of my suggested jokes as being terrible, only to watch her doing a television interview hours later and brilliantly delivering the same joke to a hysterical audience. In turn, she has roasted her husband for his overblown imagination and flights of fancy, coining the word 'Bradleyism' to describe my embroidered accounts of events that may or may not prove to be true.

Over many years together, we've shared all the successes, as well as all the knocks and setbacks. Dealing with professional rejection has always been part of our relationship. Sometimes it has consumed us. An actress wasn't cast in a film or a play, a director didn't impress an investor or a producer, a presenter wasn't chosen for a television show, a piece of writing didn't click with a sufficient number of readers or watchers, a comedian didn't get selected for a live television gala, a festival programmer or distributor decided that they didn't want to champion a newly finished film. Our professional lives have regularly turned on moments of good or bad fortune, which were ultimately just decisions made at the whim of someone else.

There has always been a balance to be struck: between ambition, the persistent drive needed to achieve, and a willingness to give up as gracefully as possible when the race is over (and someone else has won). Of course, for Deirdre and others of her ilk, being a performer is an artistic vocation, and a tough one at that. For all but the elite few, there are long stretches of unwanted and unavoidable unemployment. 'Resting' they call it, sarcastically. Then comes the anxiety when a performer is actually cast: will they be good enough, now that they are going to bare their soul in public? There is an old joke that asks the question: 'How do you make an actor unhappy?' The answer to which is: 'Give them a job.'

No matter the level of Deirdre's considerable success, we have been through that cycle a hundred times together. Many actors, singers, dancers and other performers become disillusioned, once the delicious naivety of their early careers has been destroyed by the hard realities of the industry. Plenty give up and pursue a completely different path in life, swallowing their regrets about what might have been. Meanwhile, the stalwarts who remain slowly burn all bridges and are stuck, whether they like it or not, in their own personal creative quagmires. But they are also the last ones standing, and there is honour, satisfaction and opportunity in that state of being. Not to mention the always addictive possibility that rising up over the horizon is the absolute role of a lifetime, and that all the naysayers will have to eat their collective hats when it arrives.

It was in a bid to escape the grinding cycle of artistic uncertainty and unemployment that Deirdre came to explore her talent as a stand-up comedian in the first place. Even if she has found the writing side of it difficult at times, stand-up provided her with a sense of control over her work, and it has been an amazing privilege for me to see the development and honing of that skill over two decades on stage. Nobody can find a way of shortcutting that level of experience, and every audience immediately relaxes when they sense it, through some strange collective karma that washes over them. I have always believed that stand-up comedy is the hardest art form. It's also the most primal: the closest thing we have to our distant shamanic ancestors telling stories, myths and legends around the bonfire at the end of a hard day's hunter-gathering. If you didn't hold the crowd they would wander off to an early night in the cave. If you didn't get the laughs at the comedy club it was the most excruciating and painful failure. The comedians refer to it as dying. Or, in another riff on the same theme, there is the oft-quoted but unattributed phrase: 'Dying is easy. Comedy is hard.'

One aspect of Deirdre's success that she has found increasingly difficult, and I know this goes for many well-known performers, is the public exposure in the media. It has sometimes been a case of being careful what you wished for. She has embraced social media because she feels that she is in control of it, but she has never felt the same way about all other forms of traditional media. That predicament has, at times, made her nervous, anxious and wary of the sense of intrusion. But she has always known that it's a Faustian pact – the ability to sell tickets for live gigs, successfully garner acting or presenting jobs, being recognised as a sought-after 'name' – each of them has a personal price tag.

All of which brings me back to that latest glimpse of a much-desired role, and Deirdre's attempts to capture it. Which were in vain. It couldn't even be seen as a failure, because the whole thing proved to have been a mirage. There never was a possibility of being cast; the opportunity had been pre-determined to follow another course. It wasn't even a playing field, let alone an even one. It was just another moment for us to digest together, with sadness, a little anger and a nod towards our own naive foolishness.

Then, at the moment that this complex set of emotions occurred in our household – of rejection for that particular role, feeling under siege from the pressures of needing to keep up a public profile, and inevitably having the same worries that everybody else does about family and finances – the very wind itself changed direction. One of the other projects we had been working on started to come strongly into view. In storytelling terms, there was the possibility of a catharsis that would sweep all other anxieties away, a potential reward for all those tough times.

Hope springs eternal.

WEDNESDAY, 26 APRIL 2017

I'm starting to see and sense ghosts.

My high levels of toxicity are drawing them to me.

I have to get up in the middle of the night to visit the bathroom. Not for the urgent urinary reasons that usually wake a fifty-one-year-old man. My bladder has been fixed magnificently, despite surgeon Sean Martin's disbelief that his intricate work can have been quite so successful. Nevertheless, I do sometimes have to rise from the bed to deal with the inglorious contents of my stoma bag. As I cross the landing and climb the stairs in the gloom, I am like a small child, suddenly imagining the horrors and ghouls that exist in the darkness. It's very disconcerting and I have to turn on the lights to banish them.

I ask Anne White, my cancer nurse coordinator, to meet me after I have completed the next set of blood tests at The Hospital, in preparation for more chemo. I don't tell Anne about the ghosts. Instead, I begin talking about the good times ahead. I have the twenty-first of May in mind. That is the day on which I will take possession of the Heinrich Böll cottage in Achill, for two weeks of writing and walking. I want to be feeling well by then, I tell Anne, otherwise there's no point in my going there. I argue for the physical, mental and spiritual benefits of a trip to the wild west of Ireland, even if that means dodging the last of the chemotherapy and immunotherapy, which I know is only going to take me further down, down, down.

I'm pushing against an open door. As with all cancer treatment, nothing is ever simple or sure. So there is general support for my planned voluntary exit. I undergo final transfusions of FOLFIRI and Erbitux on Wednesday, 26 April. I have completed six high-dose cycles, on top of the five of FOLFOX I underwent, in fits and starts, last year. Walking out of the ward, on that final evening of chemical cancer treatment, is like floating on air. But I have to keep that feeling to myself, as those on the daybeds around me have weeks and months to go, and solidarity is owed.

I pay a final visit to The Hospital's chapel. I have come here to sit for a few moments before and after each session. There are never more than one or two other sinners here. The peacefulness is calming and the place has a unique and interesting smell. Often I remember my sister Fiona, and I think about life, the universe and everything. I look up at Jesus on the cross. I have seen that image all my life. I remain ambivalent to it.

On the medical side of things, Dr Fennelly is anxious to have a look at a cross section of me, before he gives the final

WEDNESDAY, 26 APRIL 2017

blessing to my trip to Achill. I have a CT scan and Deirdre joins me for the results, five days later. It's another vital milestone, the importance of which the medics have downplayed again, until they are able to deliver the excellent news that it's 'all clear'. We are elated and we plan a celebratory evening at home with Holly and Daniel. Later, a fine bottle of red wine is opened and texts, the modern form of carrier pigeon, are sent all over, conveying the good news. We receive an overflow of gratifying happiness from friends and family in return.

***

My life tries to start again properly. I begin to socialise with people. They divide into two groups: those who knew and those who did not. The latter are in the majority, and I become wary of the broken-record effect whereby I will bore them with details. But I need to tell the story a little. Just to make it true.

In the beautiful month of May I drive alone to Achill Island, in a battered old Peugeot 205. It is particularly beloved by my composer friend, Stephen Rennicks, who has generously offered to lend it to me. Over the next two weeks, I send him photographs of the car parked precariously near the edge of various high Atlantic cliff tops, by way of thanks.

Heinrich Böll's remote country cottage, where I am staying and working, is warm and cosy after recent renovations. The late German novelist was a Nobel Prize winner for Literature and a regular visitor to this country, as described in his *Irish Journal: A Traveller's Portrait of Ireland* (Minerva, 1957), which sold two million copies in Germany alone. The cottage has been granted to me by The Heinrich Böll Association, which allows applicants to inhabit it for short periods, in pursuit of whatever creative endeavour they may be engaged in. It's a great privilege to be here and I feel strangely connected to Herr Böll. I commune with his spirit as best I can, while I write away at his desk, hoping for some of his brilliance to rub off on me. The sun shines incessantly outside, fading sweetly into long summer evenings. Walks are full of flitting butterflies, jungles of purple rhododendron, hoards of black-faced sheep, half-cut bogs and stacks of drying turf on hillsides, next to white flecks of bog cotton waving in the breeze.

My little family arrives for a weekend stay. We lap up the rolling surf and sandy beaches at Keel, Keem and Dugort. Holly remains an extra night so that I may deliver her to the final outing of her Irish primary school career, to take place at a water-sports centre on the adjacent Mayo peninsula.

During my return journey to Achill, a car suddenly appears from a side road and drives straight out in front of me. I miss it by a matter of feet, braking hard from a speed of fifty miles per hour. My heart is still pounding as I reach the sanctuary of the cottage. I don't need an errant driver to complicate this narrative any further.

Instead, the good life keeps on coming. I travel from Achill to Kilkenny, where Deirdre is performing at the *Cat Laughs Comedy Festival*. We have a couple of days to ourselves, for the first time in two years. We savour that luxury and further moments a week later, on our first visit to the *Festival of Writing and Ideas*, located in magnificent Borris House, County Carlow. We listen to ex-President Mary Robinson describing her gravitas-filled role as one of Nelson Mandela's 'Elders' (not being aware of her former role as one of Deirdre's most celebrated comic impersonations on stage); our friend Enda Walsh speaks about his collaboration with David Bowie in New York, not knowing at the time that unshakeable cancer would make it Bowie's last; the great American novelist Richard Ford shakes my hand and smiles with those unmistakably wise turquoise eyes; Deirdre conducts a public interview with the film-maker John Butler, whose latest feature, *Handsome Devil*, has been causing a positive stir in the little-explored school-rugby-playing-platonic-gay-love story genre; finally, we attend another public grilling of a man more usually associated with schools rugby, the acclaimed author of the Ross O'Carroll-Kelly books, Paul Howard. He is launching his latest book, *I Read the News Today, Oh Boy*. It describes the short but spectacular life of 1960s icon and Irishman Tara Browne, and outlines the theory that John Lennon commemorated his demise in a London car accident through the Beatles song 'A Day in the Life'. George Martin produced that song, although in his own books he denied that stated provenance for it. No doubt it's a debate that will rage on forever amongst the Beatlemaniacs.

Despite these enjoyable diversions, I know that it is vital for me to find other ways to calm my mind and stay mentally strong in the months ahead. Because looming thoughts about my cancer are never as far away as I would like them to be. I need to find a way to shove them even further into the distance, so that I can get on with an unobstructed life for as long as possible. I almost did a course in Transcendental Meditation (TM) some years ago, driving with Deirdre to an anonymous residential red-brick building in London's Hammersmith borough, but I bottled it at the last minute and decided not to attend. In the intervening time, I have become used to my wife nipping off to a quiet spot for twenty minutes, as she tells me that she is going to 'do her TM'. Sometimes I have been jealous of that. Even if, in the jargon of today, it has just been her way of managing to find some 'me time'.

Now I go to visit John. He lives in a tidily organised south Dublin estate, with electric gates at the entrance. He is a tall, bolt upright, gentle person and his house is simply furnished and tranquil. I have already been to his group introduction to the TM course. Now I have taken the proper plunge, paid my fees and been invited into John's home, for the first of several one-to-one teaching sessions. I have brought flowers and fruit, as requested, and I learn that these are part of a short ceremony of gratitude to Maharishi Mahesh Yogi, now deceased, who was the founder of TM. I am no part of this brief event, other than as an observer. I am pleased that I don't allow my cynicism to even enter the room.

Over several sessions, John teaches me to meditate and we have in-depth conversations about my illness. We discuss the reasons why I think I need to learn about a technique like this, and what my expectations are. We interrogate the self-discipline involved in TM, and the various claims and counter-claims that are made for its physical and psychological effects. We also talk about David Lynch and The Beatles and their experiences with Maharishi, about which I learn more later, for obvious reasons.

Meditation is a uniquely personal undertaking. I can only describe what TM is like for me, now that I intermittently practice. It relaxes my breathing and my whole frame. It helps me to escape the negative thoughts that sometimes bombard my brain. It facilitates me in finding and exploring creative ideas. It makes me interested in the concept of consciousness. Most importantly, I enjoy it and I am comfortable with it. There's nothing weird about it. I don't know why I was ever reluctant, that first time around. For a cancer patient it has been a simple and beneficial technique to tap into. I have heard it described as like washing your brain in warm water.

***

In another sign that I may now be entitled to fantasise about some longevity for myself, I go into The Hospital to have my portacath removed. This little device, under the skin of my upper chest, has been part of me for a full year. My flesh has grown around it in a desperate, appreciative hug. So it will have to be cut out, rather than easily surrendering to its removal.

I am fully awake for this procedure, which happens under powerful local anaesthetic. So I get a chance to say goodbye to it, as I feel the doctor chopping and pulling at my numbed skin. He asks me if my device has a pet name. 'No,' I answer quickly, 'but my stoma does.' It is an unmentionable moniker, provided by Brid O'Neill, my darkly humorous stoma nurse. In fact, my stoma and its accompanying Hoover bag are now the only appendages left. They are the last in a long line of invasive medical apparatus, dating back to the metal stent that mysteriously went missing from my bowels last year. I do my best to minimise the existence and the effect of the stoma on my life, and on those around me. It's a major inconvenience, and a physical oddity that I have to contend with. But I don't feel the need to talk about it, nor really even mention it. It's private and personal.

Eventually, I also get to fly on a plane again. I haven't done that since my pilgrimage to Disneyland, vaguely near Paris, over ten months ago. Now I enjoy escapades with the family to Almeria in Spain, as well as to The Cotswolds, Bath and

London, in Brexit-land. I secretly dare the airport security guards to choose me for their random frisk and to grab a handful of the stoma bag. But they never do. Even so, it remains the final obstacle to my complete freedom and I am keen for it to be gone.

So, in August, I undertake the delightful experience of a gastrografin enema. I arrive at The Hospital early in the morning and am taken straight into the radiology department by the young doctor, she of the handbag and chain fame. It is a symptom of how long I have been coming here that this doctor is now experienced, confident, unflappable and very good. In fact, she is training a new junior, and he asks me very politely whether I mind him being in attendance. Of course not, I say, as I remember a fellow patient's mantra from some time back: that we have all left our dignity at the door on the way in.

A lot of liquid is now pumped into me, through the euphemistically labelled 'back passage'. I imagine *noir* villains waiting in the shadows, on a back passage leading down to decayed docks, flick-knives ready for thievery. Also, for some inexplicable reason and with apologies to the people of Cork, I recall a place called Passage West that I visited in my childhood. I may have taken a double dose of Xanax to get through this, and that would explain the meanderings of the mind. But my own passage west is now certainly flooded with cold goo.

Then X-rays are taken of my expanded colon, focusing on the surgical wound to make sure that it has healed strongly. Finally, the goo is syphoned out, as if the villains are now stealing petrol from a car. The doctor warns me that I may have a little further discharge during the day, and tells me to be aware of that, for hygienic purposes.

This last advice illustrates the great difference between doctors and nurses. A doctor can be highfalutin, looking at the bigger picture and not always connected to the exact outcome of the battle. In contrast, a nurse is on the front line, and has seen the explosions and gunfire at first hand. In contravention of the doctor's vague entreaties, Brid the stoma nurse gives me an explicit warning. Under absolutely no circumstances, she implores me, am I to leave The Hospital. Nor should I stray more than fifteen yards from a toilet for a period of at least two hours. I listen carefully to this pre-apocalyptic admonition. I heed it without question, and I'm very glad that I do. Suffice it to say that some of the fossilised rocks that are painfully expelled during those hours definitely pre-date my second operation almost a year ago, and might actually compete with Achill turf on the carbon-dating scale.

Two weeks later I go to see my colorectal surgeon, Sean Martin. He says that the X-rays look good enough to proceed with the next treatment, and that he has been surreptitiously following me on Twitter. I follow him back and discover that he is a cycling enthusiast, one of those crazy hobbyists who test themselves on the stages of the Tour de France. That makes sense. Obviously I also think that he is a miracle-worker, whatever lunatic pursuits he may engage in during his downtime. I tell him that he doesn't need to be frightened, but that I am writing a book. He laughs out loud when I tell him its title. That pleases the small child in me. 'Okay!' Sean says dramatically. 'Let's get rid of this damn stoma!' (He actually uses some technical, medical terms, but you know what I mean.)

One more operation to go.

Stoma reversal.

Hold on tight.

I'm nearly at the finish line.

SKYING

I was doing nothing very particular, on a very non-descript Monday evening. My mobile phone rang. It was Darren Smith. Apart from being Deirdre's co-promoter on their now annual charity event, *Paddy's Night in Support of Comic Relief*, Darren was also responsible for the series pilot we had filmed for a British broadcaster earlier in the year. The initial response to it had been enthusiastic, though everything had gone eerily quiet after that. Such a state of affairs often happens in this business. Commissioning editors move on to other projects or they change jobs. Priorities and schedules of broadcasters change. Plans drift away from the ones that were best laid. Or people simply change their minds. That is their prerogative.

However, on this occasion, I could tell from Darren's voice that he was in great form on the other end of the line and that there might be the makings of a more positive outcome. He was cracking jokes, being boisterous, and was indeed the bearer of good news. Sky TV executives liked the pilot for *The Deirdre O'Kane Show* a lot. Barbara, one of the commissioning editors, had told him that lots of the British-based staff members had been watching it, laughing at it and loving it. They all obviously recognised Deirdre as an actress, from three series of the Sky-funded comedy-drama series *Moone Boy*, but they hadn't also known that she was such a strong stand-up comedian. The pilot was now, apparently, going to go out to audience research and then on to the boss man for a final decision.

Darren, who was on a roll with many other productions at that moment, was now possibly on even more of a roll, and we were very happy to roll with him. We didn't have to shoot any further footage to convince the head honchos at Sky, but we did need to spend some time working on amendments to the written proposal, while Darren and his gang at Kite Productions would hustle up further budgets, schedules and designs for studio sets.

It was a tantalising prospect, but not yet a 'greenlit' certainty. This made our professional lives hard to plan for. If the series happened it would be a coup for Deirdre, in particular, and would provide a solid period of hard, enjoyable, remunerative work for all concerned. If it didn't happen, then there would be a black hole in our working schedule and a sense of disappointment at what might have been. If we were being sensible, we needed to prepare for the latter, while not wrecking the buzz of the former. So Deirdre prepared to write a new stand-up show and I got ready to write a screenplay for Jade and Toni's film that had received some development funding. We further distracted ourselves with plans to build a home office in the small, disused yard at the back of our renovated house. We intended to call it 'Studio Two', as homage to Sir George Martin, who would be paying for it through the initial advance for his autobiography.

Unless Sky paid for it first.

If that happened, all bets were off.

FRIDAY, 20 OCTOBER 2017

It's almost midnight.

I can't believe that this is going to happen.

Sean Martin and his team have been in surgery since eight o'clock this morning. I have been on a ward, waiting my turn for the stoma reversal that will mark the end of eighteen months of treatment, almost to the day. As sometimes happens there has been a complication during an earlier operation on the rota. All other procedures have been delayed. I am expecting to be told to come back on another day. But nobody wants to disappoint me. My surgery is going ahead, come hell or high water.

As I have been fasting all day, I am very dehydrated when I come to being prepped for theatre. Outside, in the waiting area, the anaesthetist expertly slings up a large bag of saline fluid and connects it to the cannula in my vein. He gives the liquid a strong squeeze to speed the flow, and I can feel the cold rushing up my arm. In the early days of my treatment I might have found this alarming. But the anaesthetist knows that I'm an old hand, and I instinctively sense that we're within safe limits. He's like the pilot of a cargo plane, knowing that he can throw it around with more abandon than he would do if it was a passenger jet full of nervous first-timers.

At the very moment that I enter the operating theatre, Deirdre is performing stand-up comedy in front of a rapt crowd. She knows she doesn't need to worry about me. She trusts the medical team implicitly.

I have my own audience. Sean Martin and I have a laugh with some of the other surgeons and crew. We have both seen the same article posted on Twitter. It reveals that surgeons are in the top ten of 'professionals most likely to have psychopathic tendencies'. I thank the psychopaths for staying on late, after pub closing hours on a Friday night. Beyond the call of duty. Mad.

I have no nerves except for excited ones. The finale has arrived. I shuffle my stoma bag onto the surgical table for our final farewell.

The cannula in my arm sucks up the anaesthetic.

I'm getting used to this now.

Gone.

.

.

.

.

***

Later, Sean rings Deirdre to report another success. She's just finished her gig. They can't resist comparing notes on a late night's work well done. If I could give them both a standing ovation, I would.

But I am still out cold.

It is two o'clock in the morning before I am returned to the ward. When I wake for breakfast, which I am not allowed to eat, I am determined to get moving, and I don't just mean my rehabilitated bowels. After a dose of strong painkillers, I set off down my well-trodden hospital corridor routes, to clock up a couple more kilometres. I meet Sean Martin on my travels, as he does his ward rounds after only a few hours of shut-eye. We congratulate each other, passing on by.

On Monday morning I'm out of there. Ecstatic.

After a stoma reversal, surgeons leave the wound unstitched for better healing. When I change the dressings at home I have a hole in my side and I look like I've been shot. It's Halloween and I threaten to answer the door with my shirt off, fake blood dripping from what I call my 'bullet wound'. Holly and Daniel howl in disgust at this terrible dad joke.

Three weeks later I have my final CT scan of the year. It's all clear. I have no stoma. I feel like one of the luckiest men alive. Apart from that sense of euphoria, which comes in waves just like a sense of dread once did, I am able to begin the process of resuming my life completely. I have followed the advice of a writer I often meet walking by the sea. He once encouraged me to record everything about my experience quickly, before it fades and I can no longer feel the rawness and reality of it. Which is why my introductory note, about writing this book under the influence of strong medication, is not entirely a ruse.

Now I will have to mark my time in six-monthly intervals, like the age of a toddler. As successive CT scans go by, I hope to stop counting in half-years, just as older children do. Of course, I intend to be a more brilliant grown-up, this second time round.

FATHERING

Holly Bradley was born in February 2005, during snowy weather, in the same Dublin hospital where I had arrived forty years earlier. On her first night at home she would only sleep lying on my bare chest. I froze in position, too terrified to move.

When she was born we loved Holly's little form with both our thumping hearts. She followed a very late and traumatic miscarriage, which made her all the more precious to us. We would cuddle and tickle and swaddle her tight in the snuggest of blankets. I nicknamed her 'Rabbity', because of her soft hair and huggable shape, and because my mother had addressed her own children as 'rabbits' when we were equally tiny. Holly's baby-face smiled broadly when she heard herself being called Rabbity. That made me very happy.

Her first word was *hummus*, still a particular favourite to this day. We were watching series after series of the truly funny and ground-breaking comedy *Curb Your Enthusiasm*, when our daughter uttered her first, typically dismissive, full sentence: 'I don't like Larry David.' We have a lot of videotape from Holly's early years, mostly of her pointing accusingly at the lens and demanding that the camera be put away.

A few years older, and starting pre-school after we had moved to London, Holly was eager to learn. One of the concepts she became fascinated with was the phenomenon of objects falling to earth due to gravity. She asked us, somewhat forcefully, for an explanation. I did my best with an age-appropriate treatise about apples dropping from trees and a man named Sir Isaac Newton who wore a funny-looking wig. Four-year-old Holly listened intently and then concluded our conversation abruptly with a confused one-liner: 'But you call me gravity!'

Sometimes fathering is a truly terrifying experience. When Holly was a toddler and Deirdre was working abroad, my daughter slept in our bed. One night, she woke up in the early hours, spluttering some gruesome dark phlegm onto the pillow and struggling to breathe. Her lips and face turned blue as I quickly dialled 999. A paramedic arrived after ten agonising minutes and held Holly over the bath, with steam rising in clouds from the hot-water tap, to free her airway. We were then driven by ambulance to the A&E of a local London hospital. After waiting until dawn without being seen by a doctor, I took solace in the fact that Holly was now running up and down the aisles in her tiny dressing gown, with a mischievous smile on her face. I gave up our place in the queue and we took a taxi home during rush hour. Later in the day, our family doctor diagnosed a mild case of croup, which was apparently doing the rounds. Holly had a great tale to tell her mother when Deirdre returned, oblivious, from her trip. I was a nervous wreck for several weeks afterwards.

Daniel Bradley arrived in September 2008, at the Chelsea and Westminster Hospital. We knew from previous ultrasound scans that he was a boy and we felt blessed to have 'one of each'. There are early videos of Daniel too: resting in Holly's loving arms with his toothless, beaming smile, as his sister surreptitiously tries to twist one of his fingers off. Daniel has always been cheerful in the face of adversity and, even as a small boy, his knowing glances fitted the adage that 'he's been here before'. He also responded to being the second child, and therefore not so obsessively swaddled, by becoming more of an explorer and also a reckless diver-from-furniture.

Holly was unable to pronounce the name Pamela, so my parents became Palum and Papa for evermore. When Daniel started speaking he had similar struggles with diction so, for a brief time, he called his sister Colly. He had joined the family in our most nomadic phase. In order to accommodate two children, we had tried to buy a bigger flat two roads away, but our bid was gazumped by people with deeper pockets than us and with the unfortunate surname of Hole. As if to overcome this affront, Deirdre and I rented a period three-storey house close to the Thames and adjacent to the magnificently historic Chiswick Mall. It entirely suited our delusions of grandeur and probably also gave Daniel ideas above his station. He commandeered the nearby playground, which had a pirate ship as its centrepiece, and he also took to patrolling the river path proprietorially on his Mini Micro scooter. He began to attend crèche, then pre-school, and was a big hit with the girls. For some reason his mother took great pride in this, as if it backed up her assertion that she had always been a big hit with the boys.

Obviously, both Holly and Daniel travelled with us to France at the ages of six and three respectively, for the non-making of *Wayfaring Strangers*. Around this time, Daniel had the alarming habit of plunging into swimming pools at the slightest incitement from another child. He had to be urgently rescued on more than one occasion. Our children also came with us to Saigon for the making of *Noble*. Their school in Chiswick gave them a leave of absence, on the condition that we hired a tutor and that travel reports were emailed back for the enjoyment of their classmates. Daniel's education went far beyond this. He began to suck up the Vietnamese language and could always be heard saying 'hẹn gặp lại' loudly, as he trailed behind us leaving a shop. The proprietor then understood that Daniel was going to 'see you later'.

By the time we eventually returned to Dublin, Holly and Daniel were eleven and seven.

There's never a clear, uncomplicated path when it comes to telling young children about the cancer diagnosis of a parent. In our case, we decided to hold back. The only person in Holly and Daniel's family who they knew had been ill with cancer was my sister Fiona. They had been to visit her grave at a beautiful country churchyard near my parents' house in Wicklow. We often told them stories about Fiona and of how much she would have loved them. But we didn't want them to worry that the same outcome would happen to me. In those early days of my prognosis, and for as long as the medics kept giving us hope, we chose to cash in that optimism by not giving our children the precise details of my illness. Holly and Daniel had already moved country and school, leaving familiar people and places behind. We wanted them to be happy and to feel safe. They saw more of their grandparents, cousins, aunts and uncles, and they quickly made new friends at school and in the neighbourhood. As far as they were concerned, their dad had lost a lot of weight and he regularly disappeared to The Hospital for weekly or fortnightly stays. But otherwise, he just seemed to spend an inordinate amount of time lounging around in bed, where they could keep a good eye on him, and at least I wasn't able to annoy them anywhere else in the large, old rented house.

Once I was rendered healthy again, Deirdre and I felt that the time had come for a family conversation. In the appropriately, and perhaps unusually, calm atmosphere of one dinnertime, and on a natural cue in our general chat, I told Holly and Daniel that I had been treated for cancer.

Thankfully, they weren't as discombobulated as I expected. Holly admitted that she had guessed as much, because she recently saw a phone text describing me as being 'all clear'. For his part, Daniel merely wanted an explanation as to why we didn't tell them earlier. It was a relief to finally share the facts, like a lightening of the load. Although, as everyone else in the household was keen to tell me, that was the only thing that was lightening.

As my health improved, my weight was a topic that seemed to be amusing. I had proudly regained many, many pounds. Too many, I would hear my wife suggest. Congratulations on your weight gain! I would hear my doctors say, at least in my imagination. There was a lot of dad teasing going on at home. So every time I went for routine hospital procedures and scans, I told Daniel that I was going in to lose some weight. On each occasion that I returned, he would take Deirdre aside and earnestly report his observations:

'Dad thinks he has lost weight,' he would confide to her, with a discreet shake of the head and a pitying, disappointed sigh, before delivering the final blow: 'But he hasn't.'

FRIDAY, 25 MAY 2018

It's been six months since I said goodbye to the chore of having to attend to the needs of a stoma bag, and just over a year since my 'all clear'.

I arrive at The Hospital for another six-monthly CT scan. Each entry into the building brings me back to the old days, before my first operation, when I simply didn't know what even the near future held. Making my way up to the doors once more instantly triggers two of my senses. I am a version of Pavlov's dog as I hear a man's voice playing on a recorded loop over the tinny speakers: 'Welcome to The Hospital. Hand gels are provided at the main entrances and in all wards and departments. For your protection, and that of our patients and staff, please clean your hands. Thank you for your cooperation. Patients in The Hospital are cared for in a totally smoke-free environment. For everyone's benefit smoking is not permitted anywhere in the buildings or on the grounds of The Hospital.'

I take my usual last breath of fresh air and drift towards the sliding glass panels, straight past a huddle of committed smokers. (This is Ireland. We don't do rules.) Then I join a short queue of patients and visitors, all pushing down on one of the wall-mounted plastic dispensers of disinfectant. The foamy liquid stings my hands as I wring them enthusiastically, and I have the reassurance of knowing that the stuff must be slaying all manner of invisible bugs in the crevices of my skin.

I move into the vast atrium of The Hospital. This is the heart of the place, from which all corridors, veins, elevators, arteries, stairs and sinews flow. There aren't many public parts of the five-storey structure that I am not familiar with by now. I have either driven feebly along them in a bed-trolley, climbed up them in a show of strength, or meandered down them searching for a new department, where some slightly bewildering and alarming procedure awaited me. Sometimes, I have simply been lost in the labyrinth.

Compared to all that, a CT scan is a doddle. I must have had ten of them by now. The hardest part of the gig is drinking the litre of 'contrast' fluid in the hour before my allotted turn to enter the machine room. This liquid is necessary to reveal the body's insides during the scan. It possessed – until recently – a pretty vile attempt at an aniseed taste. Now some genius has solved that problem and this new flavourless solution is slipping down a treat. I bring my bottle of contrast with me as I meet Anne White in one of the cafés. We always have a gossip and a laugh before I bring up my latest medical complaints and enquiries. Anne is ever patient with her patients.

Today I report pains in my midriff. I have had them fairly consistently for a month or so now. To the point where, if I hadn't known I was coming here today, I would have visited my family doctor. Since the 'bullet wound' of the stoma reversal operation has healed, I've been swimming and walking a lot, so I'm convinced that my general fitness has improved. The news of this ostensibly healthy fact probably exacerbates the concern that I can see Anne is trying to hide. She asks me to stand. We chuckle as she gives my torso a good feel in the middle of the café, surrounded by a hundred lunching strangers. No one bats an eyelid at a sight that would definitely cause a stir in any other public place.

After the impromptu examination, Anne confidently predicts that I have a small hernia and she says that the CT scan will reveal it, if that is indeed the case. She explains that, after two major operations during which my stomach muscles have been sliced through on both occasions, as well as the impact of the stoma reversal, it wouldn't be unusual to have a slight protrusion of the gut, which is what a hernia generally represents. This conclusion actually gives me some comfort, despite the fact that I am kicking myself for not doing more sit-ups, alongside the backstroke and breaststroke. If Brid, my stoma nurse, were here now, I'd be in a lot of trouble for not having followed her exercise instructions to the letter.

I'm feeling happier as I readily drop my trousers (only so that the belt-buckle and zip won't freak out the metal-sensitive scanner) and I climb aboard the CT machine. We all know the drill by now, as the additional contrast dye drips into my veins through a cannula, and I slide smoothly through the arch of this impressive technology.

The radiologist's words echo out of an unseen amplifier: 'You may feel a hot flush, have a metallic taste in your mouth and think that you are going to pee, except you won't. Breathe in. Hold the breath. And breathe normally again.'

Later the same day, I'm breathing in the strong, salty, sea air of West Cork, consciously drawing it deep down into my lungs. Deirdre and I have been invited to the Fastnet Film Festival, in the village of Schull, a haunt of many of my childhood holidays. We attend a screening of *Noble* in a surprisingly plush mobile cinema and Deirdre womanfully hosts the Saturday night film quiz, a suitably raucous highlight of the festival. Many of my closest film-making friends are in the village for the weekend, getting involved in seminars, panel discussions and case studies for audiences of passionate film buffs. I love being with them all, being back on the circuit, being back where I belong.

But, I am anxious again.

I drink too much red wine.

I'm drowning something.

* * *

On Monday, I drive Holly and Daniel to school. It's a magnificently sunny day. Actually, it's the beginning of what proves to be another extraordinary meteorological event in the Irish calendar: a long, hot summer. There's a lot of talk in the media about the last one we had, in 1976. I was ten years old then, living in Cork, in the pink house, with the foaling donkey, the goldfish in the pond, and the dried-up ornamental gourds.

But I digress.

And, in truth, I wish I could digress some more.

I can't.

I drive on to The Hospital to meet David Fennelly for my scan results. The good news, quickly and comfortingly relayed, is that Anne White was correct in her diagnosis of a minor hernia as the source of my tummy pains. It's totally manageable and nothing to worry about. That's not the only news. David watches me carefully for a response, as he shows me the CT scan on his screen and explains the ramifications. The radiological image reveals three small nodules, two on the right lung, one on the left. They are bright white against their black surroundings. Like three little stars. Given my history, it is most likely that they are three malignant little stars.

I don't really have a response. Not disappointment. Not surprise. Not dismay. Not upset. Not anger. Not sadness. Not regret. Not panic. Not hysteria.

I feel well.
I feel calm.
I feel strong.
I feel very alive.

RESTING

Despite learning about the setback of the complications on my lungs, I'm not intending to pull back on activity levels nor make any great life adjustments. As I have no physical symptoms, I see no reason why I should. In fact, 2018 turns out to be my first calendar year in three without any form of physical treatment associated with cancer. Life is beginning to look like its former self and it is startling to behold.

Deirdre and I attend the annual *Festival of Writing and Ideas* in Borris for the second time, both as active participants. The ornate, rustic house and grounds, which play host to the soirée, bask in the ridiculously hot sun. It feels more like Monte Carlo than Carlow. Deirdre performs her stand-up comedy show, *A Line of O'Kane*, as well as moderating several conversations with other writers and comedians.

Meanwhile, I am invited to speak about the process of creating this book, nerve-wrackingly revealing the idea of it, and the fact of my illness, for the first time in front of a public audience. I finished a first draft some time ago, written for various reasons – therapeutic, diaristic and solipsistic. Having a completed manuscript, however provisional, gives me the confidence to sit in front of the Borris Festival audience and warn them that I will continue spilling my literary guts over the coming year.

In general, professionally speaking, progress is looking good as the summer months pass me by. I have signed two book contracts, made the pilot for Deirdre's television show, and am happily engaged with my chosen collaborators on three interesting film development projects.

As a family, we are thoroughly enjoying our new house. It comes with baking sunshine all day, every day. Whenever possible, we saunter down the hill and march the length of that familiar pier, stretching half a mile out into Dublin Bay, the stone of it glowing with pale pinks and oranges more normally associated with the Amalfi Coast. Or we take the children up to see the sunlit views of the coast from the top of nearby Killiney Hill. As if to prove my previous point, one vista is towards Sorrento Terrace. Then we climb down the steep steps of the adjoining quarry, which surrendered its stone to build that very pier exactly two centuries ago.

***

More than anything, after two years of solid work, and the care of an ailing husband and two rambunctious children, Deirdre needs a proper rest. My oldest friend, Sanjé Ratnavale, whom I met on my first day at Harrow School in January 1979, obliges by inviting us to join him and his family for a holiday in their native Sri Lanka. 'Paradise on Earth' it is, according to no less a travel writer than Anton Chekov. We label this generosity as the trip of a lifetime, and Holly and Daniel prepare for the three long weeks of it with building excitement. We depart just as the first rains of the season threaten to fall on our over-used barbecue.

Deirdre phones and says goodnight to her beloved mum and dad, Lilian and John, just before we board the plane. When we land in Colombo, fourteen hours later, I receive a phone call from her sister, Liz, to say that John has died during the passage of our flight. It is devastating news and the strangest of timing. John was a special man who welcomed me warmly to his family, twenty-five years ago. How could I not love him, when for a quarter of a century he called me Stevie Wonder? For Deirdre, there is some blessing in hearing that her father went quickly, and hopefully without suffering, after previous, long struggles with his health. But it is still an awful blow. It is all she can do to board another trans-world flight, writing a beautiful and funny eulogy to him on the way home. At his funeral two days later, Deirdre delivers it with grace and composure, as only she can.

We decide not to haul our children back on another long-haul flight. Besides, I am due to perform best-man duties at the renewal of Sanjé and his wife Tana's vows in Colombo, just as I did at their wedding, in the same historic city, three decades ago. I am very sorry not to be at John's farewell. But Pamela and Brendan represent me and two of his absent grandchildren. They lay flowers on John's seaside grave from Holly, Daniel and Stevie Wonder.

R.I.P. John O'Kane.

FRIDAY, 24 AUGUST 2018

The trip to Sri Lanka is over. At least I am tanned and healthy-looking as I visit The Hospital yet again, a few days after my fifty-third birthday.

I had another CT scan before I left for Paradise, and I am here to be informed of the results. The scans are now happening at three-monthly intervals. It's diligent and thorough monitoring, but it brings its own stresses. At times, I try to look inside myself to imagine what is happening in there. At other times, I try to forget all about the inside of myself. And I often succeed. Over the last month, in particular, I have been distracted by the sights of elephants, wild boar, crocodiles, black bears and leopards, as well as swims in the Indian Ocean, sups of tea at high altitude on the cool plantations and scenes of religious ecstasy at the annual Kandy Perahera Festival, as the Buddha's tooth was borne past on one of a hundred elephants, each gilded with batiks and electric lights, amid crowds of ardent believers just after nightfall.

I disinfect my hands, check in at The Hospital reception and take a seat amid a different crowd of believers in the waiting room. In truth, delays are never unreasonably long, despite what people will tell you. At the end of this particular queue is an audience with David Fennelly and my trusted oncology nurse Marie O'Brien. They are a formidable team. Somehow they continue to greet each arrival with fresh energy and focus. Marie hovers close by as David conducts the consultation, but she's paying attention to every nuance of the conversation. Her own opinions are always there when sought, and always valuable.

Today, the news from my scan is as good as can be expected, considering what we already know about the three unwanted nodules. They have not grown significantly, perhaps only by a millimetre or two. No others have come to join the party. My liver and the rest of my midriff are reassuringly clear. The nodules on the lungs are too small to take a sample for biopsy, the only point of which would be to examine whether they are possibly benign and therefore irrelevant to the war. I almost don't need David Fennelly to voice his opinion here. I know that, after decades of oncological knowledge, he wouldn't even be betting a toy house on that possibility.

We look at the options: we can 'do nothing' other than watch and wait; we can radiate the nodules out of existence; or I can undergo keyhole surgery and have them plucked out completely. I gather that the disadvantage of radiation is that you can't do it twice on one site, so you need to be certain that the nodules won't reappear in the same place. The advantage of surgery is that it should be a total clear-out and it will also provide valuable intelligence once the nodules are examined in the pathology lab. Modern medical science being what it is, this analysis can be extremely useful in designing other treatments that may be needed in the future.

We jointly decide to wait for the outcome of one more three-month cycle between scans. As I leave the consultation room I ask David what, in his considerable experience, is the range of time he expects to pass before he needs to take action. He replies that, as the nodules are not near my larger airways, eighteen months could go by before they grow big enough to cause me any discernible physical or symptomatic problems. He says that, potentially, we could 'do nothing' for almost two years.

I tell him that, if I may, I'll take that away with me as a positive.

But I also know that David Fennelly is not really a 'do nothing' kind of guy.

And thankfully, as it transpires, I'm not wrong about that.

Further action looms large.

STREAMING

Another bout of treatment is inevitably approaching, so there are realistic limits as to what I can expect to achieve in the short term. But, in truth, there are new limitations to what most writer-directors on the drama side of the television business can manage these days, healthy or not. During the last few years I've had a lot of time to think about the possibilities or probabilities of success in the industry and I have come to some clear, though not always palatable, conclusions.

It is exactly two decades since the cinema release of my first feature film, *Sweety Barrett*, starring a then-much-less-famous trio: Brendan Gleeson, Liam Cunningham and Andy Serkis. The film and television business has changed more rapidly than most industries in those intervening twenty years. New digital formats have been heralded as breakthroughs, only to be speedily made obsolete by their successors. In the 1990s, as we travelled to international festivals, producer Ed Guiney and I would board planes carrying five or six heavy reels of 35mm celluloid film tightly spooled in metal cans. In 2019, high-resolution digital images can be streamed into a cinema on the other side of the world in seconds.

Television was supposed to kill cinema; home video had been destined to destroy them both; and then it was claimed that Internet streaming would ultimately reign supreme. None of those apocalyptic predictions has yet come to pass, however. Throughout this era of ever-increasing commercial and creative churn, there has been one mantra that any writer can find comfort in, however obvious and simple (or sexist) it may seem. It is the oft-quoted phrase that 'content is king'.

Original ideas and stories conceived, written and delivered to the highest standards are the most precious and enduring commodity in the film and television market. The problem, from a producer's point of view, is that imperious storytelling has always remained an inexplicable, demanding and near-elusive art form. It has ever been thus, in all forms of narrative, since those bonfire audiences were served up myths and legends at the dawn of time.

An internationally successful film producer recently emphasised this point to me. He said that there is no problem raising funding for productions, nor securing distribution platforms in the quest for maximum global impact and success. Instead, the most difficult issue for producers to resolve is finding storytellers who have the brilliance to engage with the psychological core of their fellow human beings, while also hitting the zeitgeist in terms of marketing to a worldwide audience. In any storytelling form, locating that genius has always been an unpredictable and unfathomable stretch across the timeless. In the arena of film or television drama the hardest treasure to find is excellent, top-notch screenwriting, on any continent and in any language. Or, as Billy Wilder famously put it: 'Eighty percent of a picture is the writing, the other twenty percent is the execution.'

Nowadays, these geniuses are driving the most sought-after and popular drama content on the Internet streaming channels. Occasionally, they are also still to be found working for the traditional television broadcasters. Naturally, these authors are largely hidden from the public behind the smokescreen of the high-profile actors who front their work. But it is ultimately their writing talent that draws audiences in the tens of millions, driven mainly by that most valuable and uncontrollable of all marketing engines: word-of-mouth.

In the recent past, most aspiring television drama writers – take myself, for example – looked on enviously from the shadows when sparks from the Internet first soared into the night sky. It seemed that fresh and numerous opportunities would fan the flames out of control. We supposed that everyone could rush in and warm themselves in the glow. But, as Icarus demonstrated so meltingly, the practicalities have been considerably different.

For years, I have been researching a true-life drama that seems to fit the bill as a long-running drama series. My opening patter goes as follows: 'The epic story of The Irish Hospital Sweepstakes, one of the world's most successful organised crimes (all in the name of charity), and of the three families who created and sustained it with panache, logistical genius, violence and skullduggery.' In my head, it is The Irish Godfather, series one to seven. In real life, The Sweepstakes' stories ran throughout the world, from 1918 to 1986, in an impressive saga touching on much of twentieth-century history.

For me, it all starts with my already mentioned great-grandfather, Joseph Henry Bradley. It was he who died, with more than five hundred others, when the RMS *Leinster* was torpedoed in Dublin Bay. It was the country's worst maritime disaster. Joseph left behind a widow, Margaret, and nine young children. Into that unfortunate fray entered one Richard 'Dirty Dick' Duggan, a local Dublin bookmaker, who began a raffle to raise money for the families of the dead and injured. It was so successful, and profitable, that Duggan later persuaded the Irish State to back a similar scheme to support chronically underfunded Irish hospitals. Millions of tickets were sold through a worldwide network that was largely illegal. Those tickets were entered into a magnificently staged draw in Dublin. Each one had the remote possibility of being plucked out of a large revolving drum into which all the tickets had been placed. Those chosen few were attached to the name of a horse that would be running in a prestigious race a few days later. The ticket that linked to the winning horse was awarded the life-changing jackpot prize. But the other selected tickets were also paid large sums, in descending amounts according to the position of their horses in the race. By the early 1930s, the Irish Hospital Sweepstakes was selling tickets and dreams for three different horse races each year. In a rough calculation of today's values, Duggan and his partners in crime were grossing $300 million on each race, and paying out a total prize fund of about $200 million. The brand became as famous as Coca-Cola. It survived for seven long decades and made many people, including its promoters, wealthy beyond their wildest imaginings. For their part, the Irish hospitals received less than ten per cent of the profits, though that actually represented a vast improvement in their funding, even if it was a suspiciously meagre fraction of the golden eggs that the goose had laid in their name.

I am aware that many screenwriters have already attempted to tackle the sweep of the vast story, mostly in feature film format, but no production has yet come to fruition. I really hope that someone will succeed in mastering it, preferably as a beautifully long-running series. The question arises as to why it shouldn't be me. Which is where those unpalatable conclusions, alluded to earlier, come in.

These productions are huge beasts. At the initial development stage the producer needs a great writer who can provide a detailed storyline or 'bible' for the first series, three or four drafts of at least one episode, and outlines of where the story and characters would potentially go in six subsequent series.

That takes an enormous amount of time, energy and work. With a top-class writer, the only ones worth talking about in the context of worldwide success, this will also demand an expensive fee in order to begin the producer's gamble. (It goes without saying that this genius must then be able to take the pressure of writing episode after episode, to feed a hungry production line where hundreds of actors and crew await their scripts, never mind the expectations of the global audience and its horrifyingly immediate response on social media.)

Assuming that the storylines and pilot scripts are brilliant, the producer may manage to attract one or two red-hot stars to add to the package, in addition to a high-profile and commercially proven director to handle the opening episodes. The team will then go to Los Angeles and pitch the series to the most prominent commissioning companies with the deepest pockets. Let's say they do nine pitch meetings over two days. Within forty-eight hours either the pilot episode, or more exceptionally, the first series will be commissioned. Alternatively, if no one is impressed, the whole thing is dead in the water. In the latter case the writer is the most devastated person in the room because they have put their heart and soul into creating the drama, working night and day, and have become completely obsessed by it, possibly even to the detriment of their mental and physical health. The producer isn't too pleased, either, that the horse that he or she took a big gamble on has fallen at the last fence.

All of this is in the context of the stark reality that there aren't many of those geniuses around, in this ever-shrinking world of ours. You could probably count them on the legs of one centipede. Possibly two. Recently, I actually happened to meet one of them, walking along that ubiquitous stone pier of mine. He told me that he had been offered just such a series by one of the Internet streamers. He said that the commissioning editor had asked him pointedly whether he was ready to give up the next five or six years of his life. The writer had replied that he wasn't. End of story.

If I were a genius, I would probably have given the same answer.

Besides, I still have a ticket for my own personal hospital sweepstakes.

THURSDAY, 22 NOVEMBER 2018

I'm at The Hospital, in the office of Professor David Healy, cardiothoracic surgeon. In fact, it's one of several rooms that he is running simultaneously and efficiently, as nurses usher patients in and sit them down, with their medical files perched and ready on the other side of an empty desk. I don't have long to wait.

The professor enters briskly and takes his place in my allotted consultation room. He is reassuringly confident, immediately likeable and disarmingly straightforward. He flicks through my thick medical file as he speaks. Even though this is the first time that I have met him, his knowledge of my case is already good and he knows well what we are up against. It's an informative and calm conversation. Of course, the bit that lodges in my head is that the mortality rate for video-assisted thoracoscopic surgery (VATS) is around one per cent. I haven't been given mortality rates on my previous surgeries, so this comes a little out of the blue. But it's just a fact. Professor Healy feels it's worth imparting, or perhaps he feels it's his professional duty to say it. I presume that the statistic involves many variables – different case circumstances, age and fragility, for example – but I don't ask or comment. I don't feel the need. It's just a point of interest.

We move on quickly to a description of the forthcoming surgery to extract the nodules. It is, he explains, made a little more complicated by the fact that the lumps are spread across both lungs. Damn them. It's going to be what is known in the trade as 'keyhole surgery': five narrow incisions in total, in between the ribs and deep into the lungs. The process involves the insertion of a tiny camera, then the excision of the nodules. The surgeons will also take out a 'wedge' of lung tissue around each growth, to ensure margins that are clear of any potential cancer. More shooting and cutting. Half an hour on one side, the professor tells me, then a bit of manoeuvring to flip my prone form onto the other side. The best part is that I'll be conked out again. Oblivion is more beneficial than it is often given credit for.

How did I get here so quickly? I've had another CT scan, followed by a further meeting with David Fennelly. Since July, the nodules in my lungs have grown by a pretty insignificant margin: nothing too drastic, apart from the fact that it was growth, rather than reduction or disappearance, which can actually happen if you hit the jackpot. A group conference of my whole team was called. Decisions were swiftly made and then recommended to me. The final choice was mine. Obviously, I want us to be as proactive as possible against all continuing or newly arising threats. I have ambitions and plans for my family, friends, films and folios. And, if you remember rightly, I did previously say that Fennelly himself isn't a 'do nothing' kind of guy.

As a result of that autumnal conference, I am here meeting the professor. He is at least the sixth expert medical consultant I have referred to as mine, and I'm still counting. Now that I am also letting rip on Google, I discover that David Healy's subspecialty is in thoracic oncology and minimally invasive thoracic surgery. That's keyhole surgery for cancer patients with lung issues, to you and me. It's the very treatment that I need now. The Hospital has come up trumps once again (how that phrase seems to have lost its power in the present world).

The professor tries to explain a little of the science to me. I am now entering the realm of surgical instruments as extensions of robotic arms and computerised motion-control rigs that are employed to minimise the impact on my body, thereby aiming to produce the maximum curative effect. All of this will be under the remote control of the supervising surgeon and his or her team, of course. And if that doesn't convince me that it's a great time to be alive, I don't know what will.

REFLECTING

It is necessary to write my end-of-term report.

A summary of a moment, yet never a full stop.

I promise to keep it short.

In order to achieve this self-assessment, I am forced to suspend certain time-consuming obsessions: never-ending Brexit; fallout from the Mueller Report; a masterclass in post-terror leadership by New Zealand's Jacinda Ardern; fatal software on up-to-date aeroplanes; the admonishments by sixteen-year-old Greta Thunberg that our global house is on fire and we are doing nothing to save it; and my suspicion that every author in the world has decided that this would be a good time to publish an account of their journey with serious health issues.

I warned you at the start that I am a catastrophic thinker.

With all of that distraction put to one side, I turn my attention to this annual review and request for a raise.

I am pleased to report that only one of the creative projects that I previously mentioned has fallen. Ironically, it is *Centaur*, the book about the falling horse and its injured jockey. The director recently contacted me to say that he has decided to make the story as a documentary film. I am a little disappointed because I think I could have written a fine screenplay and I would have enjoyed the process. But the director is a strong documentary maker, with a vision for how best to tell a fascinating, true and important narrative. So I have taken his decision on the chin and am looking forward to seeing the adaptation of a brilliant book pursuing a different, and hopefully rewarding, path.

Everything else, from *The Safe* to George Martin's autobiography, to Jade's story, to Napoleon's unlikely Irish connections continues apace, and without upsetting incident, through the expected development phases. None of those projects is yet in hell (stasis or collapse), nor yet in heaven (production or distribution), but they all canter on, exciting, sustaining and stimulating me in their own inimitable ways.

There are other highs that need to be mentioned in dispatches. After the making of our pilot, and with extraordinary foresight, Sky TV has made the decision to commission a comedy series with Deirdre O'Kane, to be filmed in April 2020. This undoubtedly represents the beginning of a long, successful and lucrative partnership for the performer, broadcaster, and production company, Kite Entertainment. For my input, I am destined to receive expensive and exotic hampers from all three of them next Christmas.

All of that giddiness arises in the context of a moment of reflected glory. This astonishing event lets my progress report go out in an unashamed blaze of fireworks. My friend, best man and former business partner, Ed Guiney, has produced *The Favourite* (dir. Yorgos Lanthimos, 2018). It has garnered twelve BAFTA nominations, ten Oscar nominations and five Golden Globe nominations, a feat never likely to be repeated by an Irish-produced film. In a former life I might have been wildly jealous of such an achievement. But lately I view these happenings with an entirely different perspective. I am more proud of Ed than Ed is of himself. In some extremely tangential way, that makes it my victory too.

Overall, I immodestly give myself a B+.

TUESDAY, 5 MARCH 2019

I receive a phone call summoning me to The Hospital early tomorrow morning.

My lung operation had been delayed by six weeks, as the result of a brief nurses' strike and the necessity of isolating me after surgery because I am a VRE superbug carrier. Now, however, a possible theatre slot and a solitary bed have apparently become available in perfect unison. I travel towards them both, in another rattling taxi. It is reminiscent of my first journey here, all of three years ago. This time, I am not going into A&E, timorous and unknowing. I'm striding through the front door, by appointment, prepped and experienced. I have an undeniable sense of focus. I am determined that this surgery won't knock me off my new life's stride. I have regained my sense of adulthood and see no reason to regress this time around. I am repeating the exercise of bartering temporary weakness for long-term strength, while already desperately trying to conjure a mental through-line to the far side and beyond.

A nurse greets me with a smile. She takes me to cubicle number three to await my fate. There's nothing in the room except a television, suspended near the ceiling. It doesn't work. The universe never fails to amuse itself.

After an hour or so of solitary confinement, the nurse returns and says that she remembers meeting me before: apparently she looked after Deirdre's father, John, ten years ago. Fortunately, she was rewarded at the time with complimentary tickets to one of my wife's shows. The nurse took her boyfriend with her. He's now her husband. Bless her fine memory and the good karma she is helping to build here beneath the broken gogglebox. Her senior ward supervisor arrives next and ups the ante. 'I remember you from three years ago, Stephen,' she says kindly. 'You were so thin and extraordinarily ill. It's amazing to see you now. You look like a completely different man.' Her vote of confidence moves me.

I pace the room for several more hours. Bloods are taken and consent forms signed, as the one per cent chance of death hangs about somewhere in the ether. I'm fasting again so I don't even get to choose a last meal, which I decide to take as another good omen. Lunchtime therefore passes uneventfully, except that I am ordered to change into my surgical gown and paper knickers, and to surrender my phone, blanket and pillow, and all the other effects I have brought to comfort me after the surgery. Only the most stripped-down version of a patient can enter the gladiatorial arena.

Back in the familiar operating theatre, I strike up an instant rapport with the anaesthetist as she puts in the vein lines and attaches the oxygen. We have an incredibly interesting conversation, except I quickly forget what it was about. There's a rush of people around me: confirming my identity, age, hospital file number and, by way of a belated final check, asking me to explain why I am here. 'The removal of three nodules on the lungs,' I reply. 'It's called a wedge resection,' someone else says. 'Oh, yes, that's right,' I confirm chirpily.

Of course, there is the distinct possibility that the exchange may only have taken place in my head and I'm wondering where the surgical robot is and why I can still see the tongue and groove woodwork on the ceiling when I'm sure that I should really have gone under by now and I've been counting numbers as instructed by a theatre assistant for what seems like a very long

.

.

.

.

***

I wake up groggy, in the ICU, four hours later. I have a view across the darkening city through a floor-to-ceiling glass wall. I realise that there's an energetic party going on in my room. Nurses surround me with laughter and chatter and glowing welcomes back to the realm of the conscious. I'm as high as I should be for a man who has three tiny green 'B-lines' under his lacerated skin, delivering morphine and therefore ensuring that he is the life and floating soul of the raucous party, which may simply turn out to be the medics circling around him as they go through post-operative checks and attend to drains emanating from the surgical sites, like see-through tubes running from a beer keg at any self-respecting piss-up.

Suddenly sleep. Hangover. Exhaustion. Reality.

The physiotherapist arrives the following morning. Strangely, someone has cleared away all the cans, bottles and detritus of pizza and sausage rolls. It almost looks as if the previous night's bash never happened.

The physio gets me to space-walk again, with six tubes attached. But it's several levels of difficulty down from my previous goes. Only my long-term, core team are privy to the knowledge that I've been at this malarkey for several years now, so I can impress these blow-ins with my relative agility and superficial medical knowledge.

Afterwards, we trundle slowly to my new room, right at the heart of the ICU. It has no windows, no sense of day or night, no view of the world or the weather. Snow starts falling outside, but I can't see it. Here, on each new shift, I am assigned my own personal nurse and the care is second to none. By fortuitous circumstance, I have become firmly lodged on the most exclusive wing of The Hospital, because there is nowhere else VRE-safe to send me.

For four days and nights I benefit from this ironic stroke of luck. Despite the fact that I have a three-inch incision and a deep puncture wound beneath each armpit, my pain is minimal. As well as the B-lines, I am given another patient-controlled analgesia pump. I am under the supervision of consultant Donal Ryan, and I can't help noticing that one of his qualifications is that of *intensivist*, which is undoubtedly the coolest moniker I have ever heard and is bound to spark a television series any day now.

The cocoon of this ward facilitates my master plan. I conspire with one of the nurses to commandeer a portable intravenous drip stand. All my paraphernalia is rigged up to it with his help. These are three padlocked boxes containing morphine for the B-lines, my PCA pump and two surgical drain receptacles. They hang from the trolley like the demented elements of an avant-garde sculpture on wheels.

This artwork brings me freedom. I patrol the corridors of the ward like a bizarre post-surgical Quasimodo. On my initial foray, several of the nurses watch open-mouthed as I float by their station. I do an about-turn at the locked doors to the ward. On my return, one of the nurses explains their collective shock: patients *never* walk in the Intensive Care Unit.

I look towards the prone forms of my fellow inpatients. I have been that soldier in the past. I know that they are receiving the best of care and would wish me luck if they could. I am also convinced that movement and regaining my own strength is the secret to fulfilling my desire for a speedy return to normal.

A new-fangled, portable X-ray machine sidles into my room every day. It stretches out an arm and takes a snap of my lungs, as quickly as a teenager with a mobile phone. It reveals a partial pneumothorax, or slightly collapsed lung. I am told that breathing exercises can alleviate this problem. So I decide that it's not going to stop my progress. Nothing is.

Professor Healy collars me on his rounds. He assures me that everything went precisely as it should have during the video-assisted thoracoscopic surgery. The shooting was good and the cutting was even better. I am fragile but fixed. Now the biological samples, the surgical equivalent of film negative, have been sent off to the lab to be processed. They will tell their own tale. I thank the professor for lending me his expertise, which is the least I can do. (It is also the only thing that I can do, of course, considering the one-sidedness of our vital transaction.)

Gradually the tubes and drains disappear and I am un-ceremoniously thrown out of the ICU on Sunday afternoon, four days after the operation. I have definitely overstayed my welcome.

A small coterie of male, VRE-infected patients have taken up residence in one of the rooms on St Luke's ward and I am demoted several floors down to join them. I arrive by porter-pushed wheelchair and we roam around, searching for a nurse to check me in and confirm the transfer of my over-sized medical file. Eventually, we locate an upbeat, efficient and over-worked nurse called Jethro and I am officially handed over at the border crossing.

Once on this ward, though, my mind-set shifts. It's a huge culture shock. As far as I'm concerned, I just shouldn't be here any more. This is a place for sick people. Surely there has been some terrible mistake. I have been on this ward several times before and always found it a place of solace and safety. Now I'm finding it hard to even breathe the stale air, or listen to all the perfectly normal sounds of a public hospital ward in action. After twenty-four hours, which feels like a week, I make my escape. Homeward bound, to the bliss of my wife and children.

I'm on the oral opiates again. When they run out, I have to eat a small, shivering slice of cold turkey. There are six other types of pills to take too. Without being ridiculous or irresponsible about it, I try to forge back to full-time work, picking up where I left off. I attend social events to make sure that no one has noticed my absence. But the effects of a general anaesthetic, fatigue and wounds healing are not to be denied.

I'm still struggling vainly when I have my stitches taken out a fortnight later. During the follow-up consultation with Dr Fennelly, at the month mark, I am able to report that I am operating at eighty per cent of my former capacity.

I am here to receive the post-surgical pathology lab results.

The presence of two student doctors somehow breaks the ice.

My oncologist breaks the news.

Which is mostly good.

As predicted, the three bright little stars on my scans have proved to be three malignant little stars, rather than benign ones. But, in keeping with my initial response to the discovery of the nodules a year ago, I am encouraged to focus on the positives. The pathology results confirm that Professor Healy and his team have done an excellent job in extracting the unwanted growths, with appropriately generous safety margins. No traces of cancer have been found in samples taken from surrounding tissue. Wider tests in the lung region, like the so-called bronchial washes, have also come up pleasingly blank.

I am 'all clear' again.

There is no talk of further chemotherapy.

The beady eye of another CT scan is scheduled to keep a lookout.

But, for now, I'm going back to work and play.

***

There are hundreds of colorectal cancers, like mine, diagnosed in The Hospital every year. Many have already advanced to metastatic secondaries, where the cancer has spread to other parts of the body. I know, through institutional osmosis and the patients' grapevine, that there are some people who, far too cruelly, have not been bestowed with the biological responses and sheer good fortune that I have been gifted with thus far.

I can't explain why.

I can't quantify my own gratitude for the results of my treatment.

I can't weigh the sorrow that I feel for those patients and their loved ones.

As I near the moment when I have to stall this telling of my tale, I come upon another fluke of timing. Dr Muiris Houston, who has been the medical correspondent of *The Irish Times* for many years, was a good and valued friend to my late sister, Fiona. I suddenly spy an article in which he confronts the language that is habitually used to describe the subject of cancer. Since President Nixon declared war on cancer, Muiris says, we have progressively succumbed to an aggressive lexicon that is not helpful to many patients. A reputable recent survey in the UK has supported this contention. Dr Houston writes that 'it's a blunt message: cancer will "beat you" because you lack courage. This is absolutely unfair to most patients. The meek, the mild or those who are depressed may be neither inclined nor able to respond to exhortations to fight back'.[1]

---

1   *The Irish Times*, 25 February 2019.

Most importantly, Muiris says, it is an unjust attitude to patients who are simply not responding to treatment, through absolutely no fault of their own, to suggest that they have in some way 'failed' themselves, their families and their medical team.

The compassionate point is well made. I agree with it wholeheartedly. I am therefore genuinely shocked and a little distressed to review my own vocabulary used in this text and to discover that it is replete with the language of battle and war. I am, after all, *The Fighting Man*.

I am forced to explain myself, to myself:

When I have surgery I curse the cuts out loud.

When I have chemotherapy I rail against it.

When I can't exercise I blame my cancer.

When I feel self-pity there is no target that is out of my range.

When I write drama I am consumed by the necessity to create conflict.

When I come to the end of that, or any journey, I am looking for catharsis.

I discuss the issue with my coordinating nurse, Anne White. She has counselled and inspired me throughout. Anne tells me that there is a sense of resilience and resistance that I must allow myself, without feeling any guilt. This is not, she maintains, the same thing as aggression or disrespecting the journeys of others. I am drawn to her illustrative analogy and Anne gives me permission to repeat it: cancer patients, she says, are like body surfers moving away from the shore in order to find the ultimate curative wave. On their way out from the beach, during treatment, they try to dive beneath each oncoming wall of water so that they're not overcome by its power. If they reach the ultimate wave, they can surf it all the way back to the safety of the shore.

In truth, I am still looking for that ultimate wave. I have to accept, statistically at least, and considering my evolving history, that I am unlikely to escape further complications in the grand scheme of things. However, I am very optimistic about the treatment options available to me, in ever-improving varieties, and about the medical family who are looking after me. I may even live long and prosper. I may pour forth books, films and television drama series. Or alternatively, on a final touch of gallows humour, I may be one of the 700 who come a cropper each year, electrocuting themselves by sticking a knife into a toaster; or perhaps I'll become one of the 260 per annum, and rising, who meet their ends taking selfies in dangerous places.

Who knows?

As for the here and now, I have two revelations that surprise me:

I am without a sense of melancholy for the first time in three years.

I am anxious no more.

ACKNOWLEDGEMENTS

First and foremost, thank you to all the staff at The Hospital, my visiting public health nurses, everyone at Dun Laoghaire Surgery and McCaffrey's Pharmacy. You literally kept me going. This book is for you.

I would also like to thank my commissioning editor at Mercier Press, Patrick O'Donoghue, for showing faith in a first-timer at an early stage of the process and for giving me a wise shove in the right direction. It has also been a pleasure to work with desk editor Noel O'Regan, who improved my writing immeasurably and persuaded me to cut some very bad jokes. I am proud to be associated with this Cork-based publishing house as it celebrates its seventy-fifth anniversary. I would also like to thank Wendy Logue, Deirdre Roberts, Sarah O'Flaherty and all the other people who have worked alongside them for Mercier Press and who have contributed to the publication of this book.

Thanks to my manager, Jane Russell at Outlaw Management, who initiated the publication of this book with style and ease.

Thank you to the many friends and relations who visited,

helped and walked beside me in some of my darkest hours and happiest moments.

A special thanks to Deirdre O'Rourke for being the best of friends to DO'K always, and also to Peter Wilson (and his gang – Genny, Jodie, Andrew and Luke) for supporting my fantastic sister so well in tough times.

Among the other real-life 'angels' who came our way are Margaret O'Kane, Hilary and Donald Pratt, Eddie and Janine Marsan, Melanie Gore-Grimes and Giles Martin, Liz O'Kane and Paddy Breathnach.

Thanks to Samantha Cowap for looking after our little family so well and for keeping us all sane, and to Anne White for her constant sensitivity, advice and support (as well as for her guidance on the medical aspects of this book).

To the Achill Heinrich Böll Association, Trinity College Dublin, DLR Lexicon and Leonardo's Coffee Shop for spaces in which to write.

To Lilian, Grainne, Johnny and Noelle, Eimear and Carol – my Clogherhead family.

To Rossa, Ellie, Iarla and Donal – the future – please listen to Greta Thunberg!

To Brendan, Pamela, Suzie and Fiona – my founding family – with love always.

Last, but not least, to Deirdre, Holly and Daniel – thank you for bringing me joy.